A LEVEL MUSIC

Harmony Workbook 1

HUGH BENHAM

RHINEGOLD
EDUCATION

First published 2008
This revised edition published 2018 in Great Britain by
Rhinegold Education
14-15 Berners Street
London W1T 3LJ, UK
www.rhinegoldeducation.co.uk

You should always check the current
requirements of your examination, since
these may vary according to exam board.

Editor: Katharine Allenby
Cover and book design: Fresh Lemon Australia

A Level Music Harmony Workbook 1
Order No. RHG421
ISBN: 978-1-78558-635-4

Exclusive Distributors:
Music Sales Ltd
Distribution Centre, Newmarket Road
Bury St Edmunds, Suffolk IP33 3YB, UK

Printed in the EU

Contents

The author

Hugh Benham

read Music and English at Southampton University, where he was awarded a PhD for his study of the music of John Taverner. He is an organist and is active in the Guild of Church Musicians and the Royal School of Church Music, having formerly taught in a sixth-form college, and worked as a chair of examiners for GCE Music.

His publications include *Baroque Music in Focus* (Rhinegold Education, 2nd edition, 2010); books on English church music: *Latin Church Music in England c.1460–1575* (Barrie and Jenkins, 1977) and *John Taverner: his Life and Music* (Ashgate, 2003); contributions to *The New Grove Dictionary of Music and Musicians* (second edition, 2001), to *Die Musik in Geschichte und Gegenwart*, and to the *Ralph Vaughan Williams Society Journal*. He is the editor of Taverner's music for *Early English Church Music*. In 2011 Convivium Records released a CD of his choral and organ music (CR 011), some items from which have been published in the USA.

Acknowledgements

The author wishes to thank Katharine Allenby, Rhinegold Education Editor and Production Manager, for her help in the preparation of this book. He wishes also to acknowledge the help of those involved in the 2008 predecessor of this book (*AS Music Harmony Workbook*): Paul Terry for his many editorial suggestions, and Dr Lucien Jenkins, Katherine Smith and Chris Elcombe of Rhinegold Publishing.

Introduction

What is harmony? Why study it?

Harmony is about the relationships between notes that sound at the same time. Two or more simultaneous pitches make up, or imply, a chord. Even a single chord is harmony, but usually we think of harmony as involving purposeful successions of chords.

People sometimes think that harmony is about producing sweet sounds and avoiding anything that jars. After all, the word 'harmony' also signifies peace and agreement. But too much sweetness – too many concordant or consonant sounds – can sound dull. Like real life, music needs some excitement and tension, and this often arises from clashing or dissonant sounds. But, like everything connected with harmony, the composer must take charge and use dissonant notes in a controlled way, not randomly.

Harmony is not just about chords. It also concerns the behaviour of the various melodic strands (or 'parts') that sound together to make up those chords – that is, part-writing (or voice-leading).

Most Western music – popular, classical and jazz – relies for much of its effect on harmony. Studying and understanding how it works will

- enable you to understand more fully the music you hear, and the music you perform
- be a great help when you compose or improvise (most people would go further and say that it is essential!)
- form an important part of music courses, notably for GCSE, AS or A level, where any of the following are involved: set works, music history, composition, arrangement, or harmony and counterpoint (musical techniques) exercises.

What's in this book?

Chapter 1 contains vital preliminary information on keys and intervals. Even if you already know most of this, it is useful for revision and reference.

In Chapter 2 you will learn about triads and 7th chords. Chapter 3 shows how chords are strung together to make musical sense. Chapter 4 deals with part-writing and with non-chord notes. Chapter 5 introduces counterpoint, in which each part has more independence than in the chordal writing dealt with earlier. Chapter 6 concerns simple harmonic analysis – that is, understanding and describing existing harmony, which will help with study of set works, and will help you with your own composing. Chapters 7 and 8 show you how to write simple traditional four-part vocal harmony by adding three parts below given melodies. Such writing has been found a useful means of training and formation by generations of composers, even some, such as Arnold Schoenberg (1874–1951), whose original music is very different in style and vocabulary. Chapter 9 demonstrates some types of texture other than four-part vocal harmony, and Chapter 10 explains figured bass.

This book therefore covers most of the basics of harmony, and provides a firm foundation for further study. In Workbook 2 you can learn how to apply your knowledge to a range of tasks, including the harmonisation of chorales in the style of J S Bach.

Activities

All chapters include activities to help you learn and remember what you have read. These are not just exercises to write out. They are intended above all to help you think in terms of real sounds. So it is important to sing, hum, whistle or play everything. Don't worry about the sound you make so long as the notes are correct. Use whatever assistance you can find – ask someone else to play your work for you, use a score-writing package and its playback facility, or play four-part harmony as a piano duet – the options are almost endless.

What you need to know before starting Chapter 1

It is really important that you are confident about reading and writing:

- The notes of the treble stave
- Time values for notes and rests (including dotted and tied notes)
- Time signatures
- Dynamic markings
- Simple speed indications.

If you need to learn or revise any of these topics, please consult appropriate theory books (for example, *Step Up To GCSE Music* published by Rhinegold Education).

The bass stave

You will need also to know the names of notes on the bass stave for almost any type of exercise. If you are uncertain of the notes of the bass stave, or would like to brush up your knowledge, please read the following.

The bass stave can be thought of as a downward extension of the treble, as you can see from the music example below. The bass clef (𝄢) derives from the letter 'F' and wraps itself around the line representing F below middle C. The example shows that by using leger lines, some notes can be written on either the treble or bass stave.

You must be able to read music on the bass stave with ease, and so you may need a lot of practice. Here are three tasks which should help. If necessary, do (**c**) over and over again, with plenty of different melodies.

a Write letter names under each note of the following tune:

Sousa: *The Liberty Bell*

b Write a melody you know well on a treble stave, and then rewrite it an octave or two lower on a bass stave.

c Find more treble-stave melodies (for example, in this book) and rewrite them an octave or two lower on a bass stave.

1 Keys and intervals

1.1 The concept of key

Most music is in a **key**, with one particular note more important than all the others. This main note is called the **tonic** or the **key note** (or simply note 1) and it usually occurs frequently. It is also normally heard at the end of a piece, to provide a sense of completion, a feeling of arriving home.

Think, if you like, of the tonic as the sun and the other notes as the planets, some of which are more distant than others, but all of which are bound to the sun by the force of gravity.

1.2 Scales

Each key is based on a particular set of notes known as a **scale**. For instance, the key of C major is based on the scale of C major.

This kind of scale has eight notes. Numbers 1 and 8 are an octave apart and share the same letter name. Numbers 2-7 use all the letter names in between, once each, in alphabetical order, with no gaps.

Ex. 1.2

| C | D | E | F | G | A | B | C |
| 1 | 2 | 3 | 4 | 5 | 6 | 7 | 8 (=1) |

The scale shown above is an **ascending** scale of C. The notes C B A G F E D C form a **descending** scale of C, falling from one C to the C an octave lower.

Why is C G E A D B F C not a scale, even though it uses exactly the same notes as the example above? Because the notes are not in alphabetical order – each one doesn't move in **stepwise** fashion to the next note in the scale. Instead there are gaps, which we call **leaps**.

1.3 Major and minor scales and keys

Two types of scales are particularly important – **major** and **minor**. Example 1.2 shows a major scale. As you would expect:

- Major scales belong to major keys
- Minor scales belong to minor keys.

1.4 Major scales and major keys

How can you tell that the scale shown in Example 1.2 is a major scale? First and foremost, because it *sounds* like one! The reason for the major sound is the precise pattern of notes used. For example, the E must be E♮ not E♭, the A must be A♮ not A♭, and so on. Play C D E♭ F G A♭ B C, and you won't hear a major scale.

The notes in Example 1.2 form a scale of C major because of the precise distances (or **intervals**) between notes. If you replaced E with E♭ you would create a narrower gap between notes 2 and 3 of the scale, and a wider gap between notes 3 and 4. In fact, you would have the wrong interval pattern for a major scale.

Every major scale has the same pattern of intervals. This is why a D major scale, for example, sounds similar to a C major scale, except that it is a little higher. The pattern of a C major scale is shown again in Example 1.4.1. The letter **S** indicates a gap of a **semitone** (the smallest interval normally used in western music) and the letter **T** indicates a gap of a **tone** (an interval which is equivalent to two semitones).

Intervals will be discussed more fully later in this chapter.

Ex. 1.4.1

T   T   S   T   T   T   S

A good way to understand tones and semitones is to look at the layout of a keyboard:

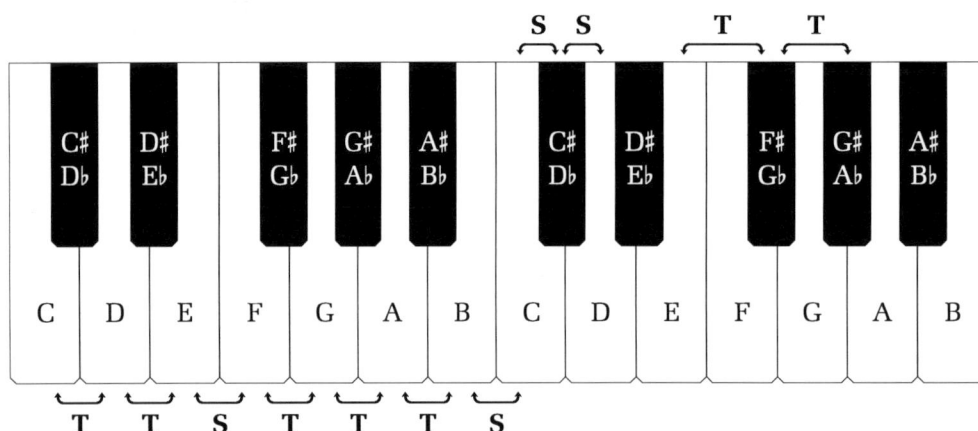

- When you move from any note (white or black) to the *very next* one on the right or left (white or black) you are moving by a semitone. The gaps between C and C♯, C♯ and D, E and F, and B and C are all semitones.

- When you move from any note (white or black) to the *next but one* on the right or left (white or black) you are moving by a tone. The gaps between C and D, D and E, E and F♯, and F♯ and G♯ are all tones.

The **T T S T T T S** pattern shown in Example 1.4.1 is the essence of all major scales. Whatever note you start on, provided you keep to the **T T S T T T S** pattern, you will hear a major scale.

Here is a complete scale of D major, with each interval marked **T** or **S**:

Ex. 1.4.2

T   T   S   T   T   T   S

Activity 1.4.1

Work out the notes belonging to each of the following major scales:

(i) F major

(ii) B♭ major

(iii) E major.

Use music notation and/or write the letter names of notes. Show where the tones (**T**) and semitones (**S**) come in each scale.

Example 1.4.3 shows the nine most widely-used major scales (see page 122 for other major scales). You should aim to become familiar with all of them as soon as possible.

Each scale is printed twice:

- In the first column the scale is shown with a sharp or flat sign placed in front of each note that needs one (in other words, **accidentals** are used)

- In the second column a **key signature** is provided – that is, one, two, three or four sharps or flats appear just after the treble clef to show which sharps or flats are needed. This is a useful labour-saving device, since it saves using accidentals, but note carefully the order in which the sharps or flats are written.

The third column shows you how key signatures are written in the bass clef.

Ex. 1.4.3

It may help you remember the relationship between major scales and their key signatures if you note that:

■ In sharp keys, the last sharp on the right of the key signature is always note 7

■ In flat keys, the last flat on the right of the key signature is always note 4.

There are three important conventions concerning key signatures:

■ The symbols in a key signature apply to all notes with the same letter name, whatever the octave in which they occur. For instance, in the key of G major, the F♯ in the key signature means that *every* F is actually F♯, whatever the octave in which it occurs

■ The sharps or flats in a key signature are always shown in the order you see them in Example 1.4.3

■ A key signature always comes *before* a time signature, not after it.

Activity 1.4.2

Write one octave of each of the following major scales in the bass clef. Do not use key signatures but add all necessary sharp or flat signs. Show where the tones (T) and semitones (S) come.

(i) F major (ii) G major (iii) D major (iv) A major (v) A♭ major

If this is all rather new to you, study the bass-clef key signatures in Example 1.4.3 to help you see which sharp or flat signs will be needed, but do take the time to learn how to work out each scale for yourself.

1.5 Degree numbers and names

Earlier the numbers 1–8 were used to refer to the various notes of a scale. But because people often use **degree names** (words such as tonic and supertonic) instead, you will need to get to know these as well:

Numbers	Degree names	Example Scale of D major	Tonic sol-fa
1	Tonic	D	doh
2	Supertonic	E	ray
3	Mediant	F♯	me
4	Subdominant	G	fah
5	Dominant	A	soh
6	Submediant	B	lah
7	Leading note	C♯	te
8 (=1)	Tonic	D	doh

The last column in this table shows the tonic sol-fa names (doh, ray, me etc.) of the notes in a major scale. They can be helpful when you have to sing, play or imagine a melody, but if you are not familiar with these names you do not need to learn them.

Note that from now on examples will not always be based on C major. Keys such as D major are used just as widely and are not really any more difficult.

Activity 1.5

a Write one octave *ascending* of each of the following scales:

- On a treble stave: E major, B♭ major, A♭ major
- On a bass stave: E major, E♭ major.

Write each scale (i) with accidentals, and (ii) with a key signature.
Label the tones and semitones (**T** or **S**) and write the number of each note (1–8).

If this is new to you, begin by copying from Example 1.4.3 if you wish. But do take the time to learn how to work out each scale for yourself.

b Write, using accidentals (*not* key signatures), one octave *descending* of each of the following scales:

- On a treble stave: F major, E♭ major
- On a bass stave: D major, A♭ major.

c Give the degree names and numbers, plus the letter names, for each degree of the G major scale. Begin as follows: Tonic = 1 = G.

d A well-known melody begins: 8 8 7 6 6 5 5 4 3 3 4 5 1 2 4 3 2 1. Write the pitches in C major on a treble stave. If you know the melody, try to notate the rhythm as well.

e In what key is the melody below? Label each note with its degree number (1–8). The final note is marked for you: 2(♯). Which degree of the scale never appears in this excerpt?

Joplin: *The Easy Winners*

2(♯)

1.6 Minor scales and minor keys

Each major key has a related minor key, called the **relative minor**, which has the same key signature. The notes of a relative minor scale can be found by starting three semitone steps below the tonic of the major scale. For example, the relative minor of C major is A minor.

Minor scales rise in steps, using every letter name once, just like major scales, and they follow any sharps or flats given in the key signature. However, note 7 of a minor scale (and sometimes also note 6) is frequently raised a semitone by means of an accidental.

Raising a note by a semitone often means sharpening it, as shown on the first stave of Example 1.6.1. But if the note concerned is a flat, as is the case with the B♭ on the second stave of the example, then you need a natural sign (♮) to raise it.

Ex. 1.6.1

If you need the normal version of one of these altered notes later in the same bar, you will have to cancel the effect of the accidental. For instance, you would need to write G♮ to cancel the effect of G♯, or B♭ to cancel the effect of B♮.

In Example 1.6.2 on the next page, (a) – (c) show the three forms that a scale of A minor can take, due to the different permutations of raising notes 6 and 7. The scale of A major is shown in (d) for comparison.

Ex. 1.6.2

(a) A minor (melodic, ascending)　　　　　　　(b) A minor (melodic, descending)

(c) A minor (harmonic)

(d) A major

In Example 1.6.2 (a) notes 6 and 7 of the A minor scale are both raised by a semitone. This form of the scale is usually found in ascending melodic passages and is known as the **ascending melodic minor**. It is very similar to A major, shown in (d), except in one vital respect – note 3 is a semitone lower.

In Example 1.6.2 (b) notes 6 and 7 are in their unaltered state (the natural signs are only needed if F♯ and/or G♯ appeared earlier in the same bar). Use of the unraised versions of 6 and 7 is typical of descending melodic passages, and this form of the scale is known as the descending melodic minor. This scale is often known as the 'natural minor' (or aeolian mode) in pop music and jazz, where it may be used in both ascending and descending melodies.

In Example 1.6.2 (c) only note 7 is raised, and so requires an accidental. The unraised sixth degree and raised seventh degree are separated by three semitones. This can sound awkward, and rarely appears in melodies. However, the type of minor scale shown in Example 1.6.2 (c) is ideal when you want to create chords. It is called the **harmonic minor** scale and is the same in both ascending and descending forms.

Activity 1.6.1

a Look at these four scales and label each one as either D ascending melodic minor, D descending melodic minor, D harmonic minor or D major. Remember that you need to look at notes 6 and 7 to differentiate between the various forms of minor scales, and at note 3 to distinguish between a major scale and a minor scale.

b What is the relative minor of D major? Remember that to find the relative minor you count down three semitone steps from the tonic of the major scale. Now write out one octave of the harmonic minor scale of that minor key, on a treble stave.

c On a bass stave, write out the complete melodic minor scale, ascending and descending, of E minor.

Example 1.6.3 opposite shows the harmonic minor scales for nine of the most widely used minor keys – first with accidentals only, and then with key signature plus any necessary accidentals. To find the melodic minor scale, remember that:

- The ascending melodic minor scale differs from the harmonic in having a raised note 6

- The descending melodic minor differs from the harmonic minor in having a lowered note 7. It only needs an accidental when one is necessary to cancel the effect of a raised 7 earlier in the same bar. For instance, in D minor you would have to write C♮ for the lowered 7th if C♯ had occurred earlier in the bar.

See page 122 for other minor scales.

Ex. 1.6.3

A minor (relative minor of C major)

E minor (relative minor of G major)

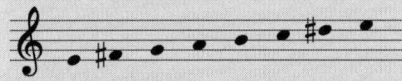

B minor (relative minor of D major)

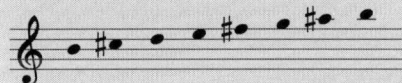

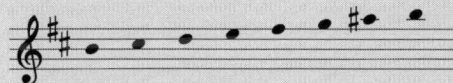

F♯ minor (relative minor of A major)

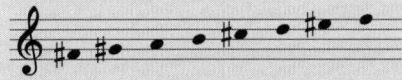

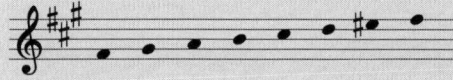

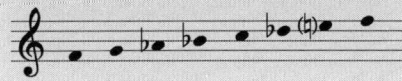

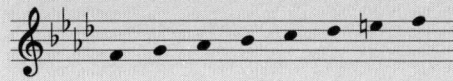

C♯ minor (relative minor of E major)

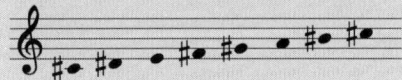

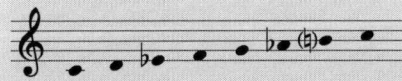

D minor (relative minor of F major)

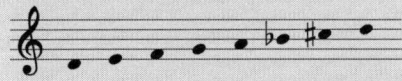

G minor (relative minor of B♭ major)

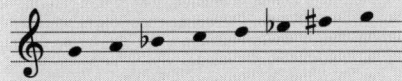

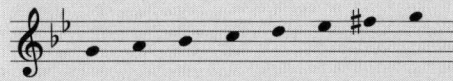

C minor (relative minor of E♭ major)

F minor (relative minor of A♭ major)

Activity 1.6.2

a Write all three forms (ascending melodic, descending melodic and harmonic) of the following scales on a bass stave:

D minor, E minor, B minor, G minor, C minor, F♯ minor, F minor, C♯ minor.

Write each scale (i) with accidentals, and (ii) with a key signature. Label each note with its correct scale number (1–8).

b Write, using accidentals, one octave of each of the following ascending melodic minor scales on a treble stave:

D minor, B minor, G minor.

Label each note with its correct scale number (1–8).

c Write a table showing the degree names and numbers, plus the letter names, for each note in the following scales:

G harmonic minor, F melodic minor (ascending), E melodic minor (descending).

Begin your first table as follows: Tonic = 1 = G.

d In what key are the two phrases below? (Notice that the second one is in the bass clef). Label each note of the melody below with its degree number (1–8).

Fred Dunn: *Jubilate, Everybody*

1.7 Two final points about minor keys

So far we have considered each minor key in relation to its relative major, since both have the same key signature, although they have different key notes.

The tonic minor

But what about major and minor scales that start on the same tonic, such as C major and C minor? They are referred to as tonic major and tonic minor respectively, and although they have different key signatures, they relate to each other like this:

- Note 3 (the mediant) is a semitone lower in the tonic minor key. It makes the interval of a *minor* 3rd above note 1, not a major 3rd, and is the main thing that differentiates minor and major scales which start on the same key note.

- Notes 1, 2, 4 and 5 are always the same in tonic major and tonic minor scales.

- Notes 6 and 7 may be the same in the tonic major and tonic minor scales, but more often note 6 (and sometimes note 7) is a semitone lower in the minor.

From all of this, we can see that the main difference between tonic major and tonic minor is that note 3 is a semitone lower in the latter.

Naming minor keys

Although there are different forms of minor scale, we do not say that a piece is in, for example, 'C harmonic minor'. We just say that it is in C minor, because composers don't generally restrict themselves to a single form of the scale.

1.8 Melodic and harmonic intervals

An interval is the distance between two pitches. If the two notes sound one after the other, they form a **melodic interval**. If they sound at the same time, they form an **harmonic interval**. Intervals are the building blocks of melody and harmony, and you must understand them in terms of both sound and notation.

> Harmonic intervals are discussed later, in **section 1.13**.

1.9 Counting intervals by letter names

When working out the size of an interval, start with the lower note and imagine that it is the tonic of a major key. Call this note 1, and then count up the notes of the major scale until you arrive at the upper note.

Look at the interval marked **1** at the start of Example 1.9 below. The lower note is C, so count up a scale of C major until you arrive at the upper note (F). You should have counted four notes (C D E F). This interval is therefore a 4th.

Now look at the interval marked **2**. This time the higher note comes first, but you should still calculate the interval from its lower note (F). Count up a scale of F major until you arrive at the upper note (A). You will have counted three notes (F G A), so this interval is a 3rd. We can be more precise. Because the note A is note 3 in the major scale of F, we can describe it as a **major 3rd**.

Next look at the interval marked **3**. The lower note is E, so you need to count up the scale of E major – E F♯ G♯. The note in our interval is G, not G♯ – it is a semitone lower than note 3 of E major and we therefore describe it as a **minor 3rd**.

Finally, look at the interval marked **4**. Is this is a major 3rd or a minor 3rd?

Ex. 1.9   Tyrolean melody: *A Man There Lived in Galilee* (abridged)

The large interval between C and D at the end of the second complete bar is a 9th (the nine notes are C D E F G A B C D). A 9th is an octave (8th) plus a 2nd. Yes, 8+2 really does make 9 in this case, because one note is counted twice when the two parts of the interval are calculated separately (C D E F G A B♭ C = 8; C D = 2).

In the case of intervals larger than a 9th, the fact that the notes are in different octaves is often ignored. So, a 10th is frequently referred to as a 3rd or, more precisely, as a **compound** 3rd. Similarly, 11ths, 12ths, 13ths, and so on are usually described as compound 4ths, 5ths, 6ths, etc. – or simply as 4ths, 5ths, 6ths.

Activity 1.9

a Look again at Example 1.9. Play or sing it, and count the intervals labelled 5-9. Explain the differences in musical effect between the small intervals and the larger ones.

b Count intervals from other melodies until this activity becomes second nature. You can use other melodies from this book, or perhaps from set works that you are studying.

1.10 Naming intervals by type

Numbering intervals by counting letter names allows us to tell the difference between 2nds, 3rds, 4ths and so on. But as we saw when we looked at intervals **2** and **3** in the previous example, there can be two types of 3rd – major or minor. Intervals of a 2nd, 6th and 7th also come in major and minor varieties.

When referring to the type of interval it is important to realise that 'major' means greater and 'minor' means lesser – a minor interval is always a semitone smaller than a major interval. This use of 'major' and 'minor' is nothing to do with the key of the music – tunes usually include both major and minor intervals, whatever their key.

4ths, 5ths and 8ths don't have major and minor versions. They are known as perfect intervals or, in the case of the 8th, simply as an octave.

Two other types of interval you need to know about are shown in Example 1.10. The lower note of the first is D. Count up the scale of D major and you will find that A is the fifth note. However, the note here is A♭ so this interval is not a perfect 5th. It is one semitone smaller than a perfect 5th and is known as a **diminished 5th**.

Ex. 1.10

The lower note of the second interval in Example 1.10 is A♭. Count up the scale of A♭ major and you will find that D♭ is the fourth note. However, the note here is D♮ so this interval is not a perfect 4th. It is one semitone larger than a perfect 4th and is known as an **augmented 4th**.

1.11 Table of intervals

Here are the most common types of interval, up to an octave. For information, the number of semitone steps in each interval is shown in column 2, while column 3 gives an example of each when C is the lower note.

Interval	Number of semitone steps	Example
minor 2nd	1 (a semitone)	C–D♭
major 2nd	2 (a tone)	C–D
minor 3rd	3	C–E♭
major 3rd	4	C–E
perfect 4th	5	C–F
augmented 4th	6 *	C–F♯
diminished 5th	6 *	C–G♭
perfect 5th	7	C–G
minor 6th	8	C–A♭
major 6th	9	C–A
minor 7th	10	C–B♭
major 7th	11	C–B
(perfect) octave	12	C–C an octave above

* An augmented 4th and a diminished 5th have the same number of semitones and therefore are of the same size, but in context each has a different effect.

Activity 1.11.1

a Give the full description (for example minor 6th or augmented 4th) of each of the intervals marked 5-9 in Example 1.9.

b Which four intervals in the table opposite do not occur anywhere in Example 1.9?

Activity 1.11.2

To learn the characteristic sounds of the intervals shown in the table on the previous page:

- Play each interval – both ascending (as shown in column 3) and descending
- Sing each interval – both descending and ascending
- Get someone to test you by playing you random selections of intervals
- Sing or play melodies which begin with, or include, particular types of intervals (for example, *Morning Has Broken* begins with major 3rd, minor 3rd and perfect 4th, together spanning an octave and making a broken chord or arpeggio).

1.12 How to identify any interval

The table in Section 1.11 listed only the most common intervals, but the principles we have learnt can easily be extended to include identifying any interval:

1 Imagine that the lower note of the interval is the tonic of a major scale.

2 Count from this note to the upper note (e.g. D to F♯ is a 3rd, G to E♭ is a 6th).

3 Find out whether or not the upper note belongs to the major scale of which the lower note is the tonic.

4a If it does:

- A 2nd or a 3rd is major
- A 4th or a 5th is perfect
- A 6th or a 7th is major
- An octave is perfect

4b If it does not, the interval is:

- Minor — if it is a semitone smaller — than a major interval
- Diminished — if it is a semitone smaller — than a perfect or minor interval
- Augmented — if it is a semitone larger — than a perfect or major interval

Look at the following melody and play it through:

Ex. 1.12.1 · Bach: Magnificat

To identify interval 1 in this example:

- Start from the *lower* note (E) and count up the scale of E major
- Note 2 of E major is F♯, so this is some kind of 2nd
- E–F♯ would be a major 2nd, but the upper note in our interval is F♮, a semitone below F♯. The interval is a semitone smaller than a major 2nd – it must therefore be a **minor 2nd**. Remember: the interval is minor if it is a semitone smaller than a major interval.

Interval **2** is a 6th. Because G is the lower note, think in terms of the G major scale. Does this scale have an E? Yes. So this interval is a **major 6th**.

Now look at interval **3**. As always, remember to count from the lower note (B♭). The scale of B♭ major has C as its second note, so B♭–C would be a major 2nd. The interval here (B♭–C♯) is a semitone larger, so this interval is an **augmented 2nd**.

Ex. 1.12.2 — Bach: Prelude in C major, BWV 846
Ex. 1.12.3 — Bach: Prelude in C major, BWV 846

In Example 1.12.2 every bracketed interval is the same because the effect of the sharp lasts throughout the bar. G to C would be an interval of a perfect 4th, but here we have G to C♯, which is one semitone larger. It is therefore an **augmented 4th**.

Similarly, in Example 1.12.3, the effect of the E♭ lasts throughout the bar, so both bracketed intervals are the same. A to E would be a perfect 5th, but here we have A to E♭, which is one semitone smaller, making this a **diminished 5th**.

Ex. 1.12.4 — Handel: *Messiah*

Finally, the bracketed interval in Example 1.12.4 is a **diminished 7th**. E♮ is the lower note (notice the music is in the bass clef). In the key of E major, E–D♯ would be a major 7th. The interval a semitone smaller (E–D♮) would be a minor 7th. But our interval is a semitone smaller still (E–D♭). It must be diminished, because an interval is diminished if it is a semitone smaller than a minor interval.

Activity 1.12

a Identify intervals **4** and **5** in Example 1.12.1, on the previous page.

b Identify intervals from as many other melodies in this book as possible.

c Using a treble stave and a key signature of G major, write the following pitches. They form the start of a well-known tune: try to add the rhythm if you can.

Begin with D (a tone above middle C) and repeat it.
Move up a major 2nd (to E), and then back to D.
Next go up a perfect 4th, and then down a minor 2nd.
Now go down a major 3rd and repeat this note.
Move up a major 2nd, down a major 2nd, up a perfect 5th and down a major 2nd.

1.13 Harmonic intervals

Notes sounded together form harmonic intervals, and these are calculated and named in just the same way as melodic intervals, counting up from the lower note. In Example 1.13.1, the first interval is a major 3rd and the second is a minor 3rd. Notice that the notes in harmonic intervals are sometimes written with a single stem and sometimes with separate stems in opposite directions.

Example 1.13.2 shows an 'interval' we haven't mentioned before – two different parts playing or singing the same pitch. This is known as a **unison**. Notice that if the notes are semibreves there are no stems to point in different directions, so the semibreves are staggered. They should *just* touch.

Staggered note-heads are also needed when writing a 2nd as an harmonic interval. Look carefully at Example 1.13.3. Stems always go between the two note-heads of a 2nd, whatever their direction. If accidentals are needed they are always written before the complete interval, with the lower one first if there are two.

Ex. 1.13.1

Ex. 1.13.2

Ex. 1.13.3

Sometimes the notes in an harmonic interval are on different staves. The method is no different – just remember how the bass and treble staves overlap and count in the usual way. Interval **1** in Example 1.13.4 is a perfect 5th. Interval **2** is a unison, because both notes are middle C. Try naming the other intervals.

Ex. 1.13.4

Activity 1.13

Name the harmonic intervals **1–10** in the music below. Ignore the difference in octaves for intervals larger than a 9th – for example, the note marked * could be described as a (compound) minor 6th. Notice that new harmonic intervals can be created when a previous note hangs on, as shown by the lines in intervals **8** and **10**.

Vivaldi: Sonata in C minor

1.14 Writing intervals

The method for identifying intervals will work just as well if you have to write an interval *above* a given note. For instance, if you want to write a minor 3rd above G, count three notes up the scale of G major (to B). This will give you the major 3rd, so then lower the upper note by a semitone (to B♭) to form the minor 3rd.

If you want to write an interval *below* a given note, such as a major 3rd beneath G, first count down 3 letter names (G F E). Then, in the usual way, count 3 notes up the scale of E major to see if you arrive back on G. You don't! You arrive on G♯, a semitone too high. Since G is fixed, move the *lower* note down a semitone, to E♭. Confirm that this is right by counting up a scale of E♭ major to check that note 3 is G.

Activity 1.14

Add a note to each of the following to make the named harmonic intervals:

2 Chords

A chord is heard when two or more notes are sounded together. Since about 1900 some composers have formed chords from almost any combination of notes. Before this, people generally relied on a smallish number of familiar chords, all of which are still widely used today, not least in popular music and film music. We need to learn about them to be able to understand how the harmony works in pieces that we study, and how to write harmony of our own.

2.1 Triads

The most widely used type of chord is the **triad**. The very word 'tri-ad' suggests that three notes are involved. However, a triad cannot be any combination of three notes. The triads in Example 2.1 contain two 3rds, one on top of the other. But we can also describe them like this:

Ex. 2.1

- The top note is a 5th above the bottom note   bottom to top = 5
- The middle note is a 3rd above the bottom note   bottom to middle = 3

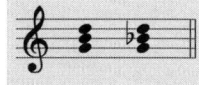

The chords in Example 2.1 are triads in their most basic form. The intervals are a 5th and a 3rd above the bottom note, which is known as the **root**, and so each triad here is said to be in **root position**, and can be described as a $\frac{5}{3}$ ('five-three') chord.

2.2 Types of triads

There are four types of $\frac{5}{3}$ chord – major, minor, diminished and augmented – although major and minor are by far the most common:

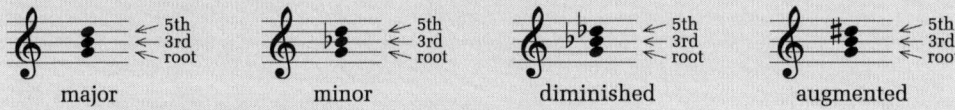

The root of a $\frac{5}{3}$ chord is its foundation and its most vital part. The middle note is called the 3rd because it is a 3rd above the root and the top note is called the 5th because it is a 5th above the root.

Every major triad has:

- A *perfect* 5th between the root and the 5th
- A *major* 3rd between the root and the 3rd.

Every minor triad has:

- A *perfect* 5th between the root and the 5th
- A *minor* 3rd between the root and the 3rd.

Every diminished triad has:

- A *diminished* 5th between the root and the 5th
- A *minor* 3rd between the root and the 3rd.

Every augmented triad has:

- An *augmented* 5th between the root and the 5th
- A *major* 3rd between the root and the 3rd.

Diminished and augmented triads are uncommon largely because their diminished and augmented 5ths make them sound less settled than major and minor $\frac{5}{3}$ chords.

A triad is usually referred to by its root note and type. So the four triads identified in Example 2.2 are G major, G minor, G diminished and G augmented.

To work out what notes belong to a particular major or minor $\frac{5}{3}$ chord, you need to know that:

- A major $\frac{5}{3}$ chord consists of notes 1, 3 and 5 of the major scale that starts on the root. For example, a triad of E♭ major consists of E♭ G B♭.

- A minor $\frac{5}{3}$ chord consists of notes 1, 3 and 5 of the minor scale that starts on the root note. For example, a triad of F minor consists of F A♭ C.

After a while, you won't have to work each triad out from scratch every time. You'll begin to remember, for example, that an A major $\frac{5}{3}$ chord is A C♯ E.

Activity 2.2

a Play the four triads in Example 2.2 (on the previous page) as chords and then play them melodically (each note separately). Sing the melodic versions. Can you hear the differences between them?

b Ask someone to play some more triads so that you can get really good at spotting the different types.

c Identify the triads marked * on staves (i) and (ii) below. In each case, label the root 'R', the 3rd '3' and the 5th '5'. For example, the first $\frac{5}{3}$ chord in (i) is F major, with F being 'R', A being '3' and C being '5'. Use your ears as well as your eyes!

Handel: *Judas Maccabaeus* (adapted)

John L Bell: *Glory to God Above!*

d Write the following *major* triads on a treble stave and label the notes R, 3 and 5: C, G, A, B♭, E, D, A♭.

e Write the following *minor* triads on a treble stave and label the notes R, 3 and 5: E, A, B, F, G, C, D.

2.3 Triads in first inversion

The triads discussed so far are said to be in **root position**, because the root is the lowest note. If you alter the order of the notes so that the root is no longer at the bottom, you create an **inversion**. Look at the chord marked **X** on stave (i) above. It is a chord of F major (F A C) but the lowest note is A, not F. It is an inverted chord.

Now look at the first chord in Example 2.3.1. It is a G major triad. If you juggle the notes so that the G flips up an octave, leaving B at the bottom, you have a triad of G major in **first inversion**.

Ex. 2.3.1

5   first
3   inversion

The intervals in first-inversion chords follow this pattern:

- The top note is a 6th above the bottom note   bottom to top = 6
- The middle note is a 3rd above the bottom note   bottom to middle = 3

This explains why first inversions are referred to as $\frac{6}{3}$ chords. The first inversion chord in Example 2.3.1 consists of B D G. G is a 6th above B, and D is a 3rd above B.

The descriptions of the notes in a chord do not change when it is inverted. As you can see in Example 2.3.2, the root is still the root, the 3rd is still the 3rd, and the 5th is still the 5th. What is different is that **the root is no longer the lowest note when a chord is inverted**. Be very careful over this point.

Ex. 2.3.2

Activity 2.3

a Play again the major and minor triads in Example 2.1 on page 20. Play them as chords and melodically (that is, with notes separately). Sing the melodic versions. Then play and sing the same chords as first inversions, again both as chords and melodically. Are you sure of the differences in sound between major and minor triads and the first inversions which contain the same notes?

b Ask someone to play more $\frac{5}{3}$ and $\frac{6}{3}$ chords so that you get really good at spotting the difference. Concentrate on majors and minors, with a few diminished.

c Find, and then name, each $\frac{6}{3}$ chord in the following quotation. Label the root 'R' in each case. For example, the first $\frac{6}{3}$ chord is the first inversion of C major in the second half of bar 1. Its root is C at the top of the chord.

Don't forget that this means B is B♭ throughout the bar

Bernstein: 'America' from *West Side Story* (upper parts)

d Write, on a treble stave, the following *major* triads in $\frac{6}{3}$ position and label the root as 'R' in each one. The answer to the first chord is: A C F (R=F).
F, D, A, B♭, E, A♭, E♭.

e Identify the following major and minor triads in $\frac{6}{3}$ position and label the root as 'R' in each one. The answer to the first chord is given.

E minor

2.4 Triads in second inversion

Earlier we juggled G B D so that it became B D G (see Example 2.3.1 on page 21).

Now continue juggling, so that the B of B D G flips up an octave to the top of the chord and D is at the bottom.

This creates a triad in **second inversion** (D G B), shown in Example 2.4.1.

Ex. 2.4.1

The intervals in second-inversion chords follow this pattern:

■ The top note is a 6th above the bottom note   bottom to top = 6
■ The middle note is a 4th above the bottom note   bottom to middle = 4

This explains why second inversions are referred to as $\frac{6}{4}$ chords. The second-inversion chord in Example 2.4.1 consists of D G B. B is a 6th above D, and G is a 4th above D.

Remember, the descriptions of the notes in a chord do not change when the chord is inverted. As you can see in Example 2.4.2, the root is still the root, the 3rd is still the 3rd, and the 5th is still the 5th:

Ex. 2.4.2

Wagner: *Tannhäuser*

Take careful note of this important tip:

$\frac{6}{4}$ chords are used *much* less frequently than $\frac{5}{3}$ and $\frac{6}{3}$ chords in the styles of music discussed in this book. Many mistakes in harmony coursework and exam papers arise from overuse of $\frac{6}{4}$ chords.

Activity 2.4

a Play again the major and minor triads in Example 2.1 on page 20. Play them as chords and melodically (that is, with notes separately). Sing the melodic versions. Then play and sing the same chords as second inversions, again both as chords and melodically. Are you sure of the differences in sound between major and minor triads and the second inversions which contain the same notes?

b Ask someone to play some more $\frac{5}{3}$, $\frac{6}{3}$ and $\frac{6}{4}$ chords so that you get really good at spotting the differences.

c Find, and then name, each $\frac{6}{4}$ chord in the following passage. Label the root 'R' in each case. The first answer has been given.

W P Rowlands: *Blaenwern* (adapted)

d Identify the following major and minor triads in $\frac{6}{4}$ position, and label the root as 'R' in each one. Notice that chords in bars 4 and 5 are spread across two staves. The answer to the first chord is given.

> Unsure of the answers to the last two chords? Check the table of more unusual keys on page 122.

e Write, on a *bass* stave, the following triads in $\frac{6}{4}$ position and label the root as 'R' in each one:

C major, D major, E♭ major, F minor, G minor, A major.

2.5 Root-position triads in major keys

Triads function within keys, which they in turn help to establish and maintain.

Each triad in a key can be called by the name or number of the scale degree of its root. For instance, a D major triad in the key of D major is the tonic triad because it has the tonic note (1) of the key as its root. As shown in Example 2.5.1, a G major triad is the dominant triad in the key of C major because it has the dominant note (5) of the key as its root.

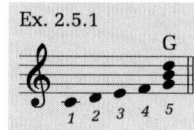

Ex. 2.5.1

It is quicker to use numbers to identify triads. We employ Roman numerals (I, II etc.) for this purpose instead of the Arabic numbers (1, 2 etc.) used for degrees of the scale. So chord I is another name for the tonic triad, chord V for the dominant triad, and so on. To put it another way, chord I has note 1 as its root, chord V is built on note 5, etc.

Chords can also be labelled with the symbols used in jazz and popular music:

- Major triads have the letter names of their roots
  Example: D means a D major chord
- Minor triads have the letter names of their roots plus 'm' for minor
  Example: Em means an E minor chord
- Diminished triads have the letter names of their roots plus 'dim' (or ^{O})
  Example: E dim or E^O means a diminished chord on E
- Augmented triads have the letter names of their roots plus 'aug' (or $^+$)
  Example: F aug or F$^+$ means an augmented chord on F.

The following table gives the complete set of seven triads for the key of D major, one for each degree of the scale.

Note the following points, which apply to chords in *all* major keys:

- There are three major triads (I, IV and V). These are known as the **primary triads**. Two of them, I and V, are particularly important in establishing the key.
- There are three minor triads (ii, iii and vi) in every major key. Their numbers are printed in lower-case type to remind you that they are minor.
- The triad on the leading note (*vii*) is a diminished triad. The Roman numerals of diminished chords are printed in lower-case *italic* type in this book.

Scale degree	Scale number	Chord number	Type of triad	Chord name and notes in D major	
Tonic	1	I	**major**	D	D F♯ A
Supertonic	2	ii	minor	Em	E G B
Mediant	3	*iii*	minor	F♯m	F♯ A C♯
Subdominant	4	IV	major	G	G B D
Dominant	5	V	**major**	A	A C♯ E
Submediant	6	vi	minor	Bm	B D F♯
Leading note	7	*vii*	diminished	C♯dim	C♯ E G

Here are examples of all seven chords in the key of D major:

Ex. 2.5.2

Activity 2.5

a Write chord tables similar to the one on the previous page for at least four other major keys (for instance, C, F, G and B♭).

b On a treble stave, write triads I and V in C major, E♭ major, A major and B♭ major.

c On a bass stave, write triads I and V in F major, G major, D major and A♭ major.

d This is an exercise to help you think fairly quickly in a variety of keys. Begin by playing an F major scale. Then play triads I, V and I again in F major. Next play a different major scale (perhaps G major) followed by triads I V I. Do the same in other major keys.

What you've just done is to **transpose** chords from one key to another. Such transposition is the best way of getting to understand the relationships between keys and chords.

2.6 First-inversion triads in major keys

Here are the triads of D major in first inversion. When using Roman numerals, the letter 'b' is often added to indicate a first-inversion ($\frac{6}{3}$) chord. (Technically, root-position chords are in position 'a' – Ia, Va and so forth – but the 'a' is not normally included). When using chord names, the lowest note of the chord is shown after a slash symbol if the chord is not in root position:

You may sometimes see first-inversion chords referred to in the style I$\frac{6}{3}$ or I^6, etc.

Activity 2.6

a Write chord tables similar to the one on the previous page for first-inversion chords in at least four other major keys (for instance, C, F, G and B♭).

b On a treble stave, write chords Ib and Vb in the keys of C major, E♭ major, A major and B♭ major.

c On a bass stave, write chords Ib and Vb in the keys of F major, G major, D major and A♭ major.

d Here is another exercise in transposition. Begin by playing an F major scale. Then play chords Ib, *viib*, Ib, iib in F major. Now play a different major scale (perhaps G major) followed by chords Ib, *viib*, Ib, iib. Do the same in other major keys.

2.7 Second-inversion triads in major keys

A letter 'c' is placed after the Roman numeral to indicate a second-inversion chord. When using chord names, the lowest note is shown after a slash symbol if the chord is not in root position.

Chord Ic (sometimes referred to as I$\frac{6}{4}$) is the only $\frac{6}{4}$ chord that we need to identify at present: it is shown in the key of D major in Example 2.7.

Activity 2.7

a Using a treble stave, write chord Ic in each of the following major keys:
F, B♭, C, A, E, G.

b Identify the key and chord (including correct inversion) of each of the following tonic triads.
They include chords I, Ib and Ic. The first answer is given.

Ic
C major

2.8 Root-position triads in minor keys

As you already know, minor scales are variable in a way that major scales are not.
For example, scales of D minor always begin D E F G A – they may then have B♮ or B♭,
and C or C♯.

Accordingly, no fewer than 13 triads are available in each minor key, because the chords
that contain note 6 or note 7 (which means all chords except the tonic) exist in two different
versions. For example in D minor, the chord on the second note of the scale (E) can be E G B
(the minor triad ii) or E G B♭ (the diminished triad *ii*).

> At the *end* of a piece In a minor key, even chord I is sometimes altered –
> to include a *major* 3rd above the root (a **tierce de Picardie** – see section 3.19).

But when you come to work harmony exercises, you will more often than not use **chords
based on the harmonic minor scale** – in D minor this means B♭ and C♯ rather than B♮ and C.
In the following table, note that:

- Major triads occur in minor keys, just as minor triads occur in major keys

- The primary triads are i, iv and V, as they are in major keys, but notice that i and iv are
  minor, while V is major

- Once again, chords i and V are absolutely vital in establishing the key.

Scale degree	Scale number	Chord number	Type of triad	Chord name and notes in D minor	
Tonic	1	i	minor	Dm	D F A
Supertonic	2	*ii*	diminished	Edim	E G B♭
Mediant	3	*III*	augmented	Faug	F A C♯*
Subdominant	4	iv	minor	G	G B♭ D
Dominant	5	V	major	A	A C♯ E
Submediant	6	VI	major	B♭	B♭ D F
Leading note	7	*vii*	diminished	C♯dim	C♯ E G

* see note on next page

Here are examples of all seven chords in the key of D minor:

Ex. 2.8

Dm	Edim	Faug or F	Gm	A	Bb	C#dim
i	ii	III* or III	iv	V	VI	vii

* The augmented version of the triad on the mediant is rare. The lowered version of note 7 is more commonly used in this chord, thus making it a major triad. For example, in the key of D minor, chord III is usually F A C rather than F A C#.

Activity 2.8

a Write chord tables similar to the one above for at least four other minor keys (for instance, A minor, G minor, E minor, and C minor).

b On a treble stave, write chords i and V in the keys of A minor, C minor, F minor and F# minor. Remember to include all necessary accidentals.

c On a bass stave, write chords i and V in the keys of E minor, G minor, B minor and D minor. Remember to include all necessary accidentals.

d This is another exercise in transposition. Play the scale of A harmonic minor. Then play chords i, V and i in A minor. Next play a different minor scale (perhaps G minor) plus chords i, V and i in that key. Do the same in other minor keys.

2.9 First-inversion and second-inversion triads in minor keys

Here are the first-inversion triads in D minor. As we noted in the previous section, we will be using mainly chords based on the harmonic minor scale, but remember that the different possibilities for notes 6 and 7 in the minor scale mean that you will sometimes encounter various other versions of all chords except the tonic.

Ex. 2.9.1

Dm/F	Edim/G	Faug/A or F/A	Gm/Bb	A/C#	Bb/D	C#dim/E
ib	iib	IIIb or IIIb	ivb	**Vb**	VIb	viib

Chord Ic is the only second-inversion triad that we need to identify at present: it is shown in the key of D minor in Example 2.9.2.

Ex. 2.9.2

Dm/A

Ic

2.10 Identifying inverted chords

To find the letter name of an inverted triad, keep moving its top note down an octave until the notes of the chord are *all* on either lines or spaces. This will give you the chord in root position, thus enabling you to name it:

Ex. 2.10

E minor
all notes on lines

E minor
6
4

D major
all notes on spaces

D major
6
3

Activity 2.10

Label each of the following chords with a Roman numeral and (where necessary) an inversion letter, and/or with the correct chord name (e.g. Gm/B♭). Keys are given.

2.11 7th chords

A $\frac{5}{3}$ contains two 3rds, one on top of the other. If we extend the pile of 3rds to three, we get a 7th chord, so called because there is an interval of a 7th between the root and the top note.

The intervals in 7th chords follow this pattern:

- The top note is a 7th above the root   bottom to top = 7
- The second highest note is a 5th above the root   bottom to middle = 5
- The second lowest note is a 3rd above the root   bottom to second lowest = 3

The 7th chord in Example 2.11.1 is A^7 (a chord of A major plus a 7th) and it consists of A, C♯ a 3rd higher, E a 3rd higher still, and G a 3rd higher again.

You can build a 7th chord by adding an additional 3rd above any root-position triad, but the two most common are those on notes 2 and 5 of the scale – the **supertonic 7th** (ii^7) and the **dominant 7th** (V^7). Here they are in the keys of D major and D minor:

There are several things to notice about these chords:

- Chord V^7 is exactly the same in the tonic minor as it is in the tonic major key
- The 7th in all four chords printed here is a *minor* 7th above the root
- The triads below each 7th are the same as those we learned earlier – V is major, while ii is a minor triad in major keys, but a *diminished* triad in minor keys.

The '♭5' in the chord notation for Em$^{7♭5}$ reflects the diminished 5th in the chord. This type of chord is sometimes called a 'half-diminished 7th' – half, because the 5th is diminished but the 7th is not. You may see this chord notated as E^ø or E^{ø7}.

Diminished 7th chords will be discussed on the next page.

Activity 2.11

a On a treble stave write chords ii^7 and V^7 in the following keys:
C major, E♭ major, A minor and F minor.

b On a bass stave write chords ii^7 and V^7 in the following keys:
G major, B♭ major, E minor and C minor.

2.12 Inverting 7th chords

7th chords are inverted in exactly the same way as triads but, because they have four notes, there are *three* possible inversions instead of two. V⁷ may appear in any inversion, but ii⁷ and ii⁷ are most often seen in first inversion.

Ex. 2.12

| C⁷ | C⁷/E | C⁷/G | C⁷/Bb | Gm⁷ | Gm⁷/Bb |

F major: V⁷ root position · V⁷ first inversion · V⁷c second inversion · V⁷d third inversion · ii⁷ root position · ii⁷b first inversion

To identify a 7th chord, use the method described in **Section 2.10** on page 27 – rearrange the notes so they are *all* on either lines or spaces. This will give you the chord in root position, thus enabling you to name it.

Activity 2.12

Identify each of the following chords as either ii⁷ or V⁷ and indicate the inversion if the chord is not in root position. The first answer is given.

C major · G major · A minor · F major · Bb major · B minor

V⁷b

2.13 The diminished 7th chord

As mentioned in the previous section, 7th chords can be built on any note of the scale. The dominant 7th and supertonic 7th are the most common, but there is one other type you need to know about now, and that is the 7th chord on the leading note, chord *vii⁷*. Here it is in D minor, and then in D major:

Ex. 2.13.1 — D minor — C#dim 7 — vii⁷ — D major — C#m⁷b5 — vii⁷

Let's look at the minor-key version first this time. In minor keys, chord *vii⁷* is a diminished 7th – so called because there is an interval of a diminished 7th between the root and the upper note. It is easy to form a diminished 7th chord if you remember that each note is a minor 3rd higher than the previous one. You may sometimes see the chord symbol for a diminished 7th printed as ᵒ⁷ (for example, C#ᵒ⁷).

In major keys, chord *vii⁷* consists of two minor 3rds plus a *major* 3rd. This means that it includes the same diminished 5th between root and 5th as vii⁷ in a minor key, but the 7th itself is a *minor* 7th, not a diminished 7th, above the root. It is, in fact, the same type of half-diminished 7th that we saw on the previous page. Remember, you may see the chord name for the half-diminished 7th expressed in the form C#ø.

Example 2.13.2 shows the same two chords as Example 2.13.1, but an octave lower.

To summarise the difference between diminished and half-diminished 7th chords:

- A **diminished 7th** consists of a minor 3rd, diminished 5th and diminished 7th above the root

- A **half-diminished 7th** consists of a minor 3rd, diminished 5th and minor 7th above the root.

Ex. 2.13.2

Activity 2.13

Write the chord indicated above each of the following notes. A tip: in this exercise, the note of each chord should either be all on lines or else all on spaces since every chord is in root position. Remember to play everything you write, either as a complete chord or by sounding the notes melodically.

2.14 Chords in open position

So far we have kept the notes of each chord as close together as possible (in what is called **close position**). It is time now to find out how to spread the notes of a chord out over a wider range (in **open position**).

To do this, notes can be moved up or down by one or more octaves, and the order of the upper notes can be changed. But there is one vital rule:

- **The lowest note of the chord**, whether it is root, 3rd, 5th or 7th, **must always remain the lowest note**.

Here is a root-position triad of F major, first in close position and then in various open spacings. Notice that the lowest note is always F, whatever the order of the upper notes.

Ex. 2.14.1

This principle holds good for inversions. The first stave in Example 2.14.2 shows a $\frac{6}{3}$ chord of F major in close position, followed by various open spacings. In each one, the 3rd (A) remains the lowest note.

Ex. 2.14.2

And the same principle applies to other chords, such as $\frac{6}{4}$ and 7th chords, and their various inversions. Here are a few examples:

Ex. 2.14.3

close open close open close open close open

5th

5th root

root

root

3rd

3rd

root

root

F second inversion   C⁷ root position   F⁷ first inversion   Diminished 7th

Despite all these different possibilities, the method for identifying chords in open position is very similar to the way we learned earlier:

- Rearrange the chord so that it is in close position and with all its notes on either lines or on spaces. The chord is then in root position and can be named.

- From this, you can work out if the original chord is in root position or which inversion it is in.

Ex. 2.14.4

Cm⁷

This method is illustrated in Example 2.14.4. The first chord has been rearranged into close position, with all notes on lines, by moving the bass-clef E♭ up an octave. This allows us to see that the chord is Cm⁷. In the original chord, the 3rd (E♭) is in the bass, so we can now say that it is Cm⁷ in first inversion.

Activity 2.14

a On a pair of staves (treble and bass) write two different open-position spacings for the root-position triads of E minor and G major. You can space your chords as you wish, but avoid too much use of leger lines. Then write two open-position spacings for the first and second inversions of the same chords.

b On a similar pair of staves, write two different open-position spacings of each of the following chords:

- G⁷ in root position, first inversion and third inversion

- Dm⁷ in root position and first inversion.

c Fully identify each of the chords below. If you use Roman numerals, add a letter to show any inverted chords. If you use chord names, show any inversions with 'slash-chord' notation (for example, Cm/G). The key is G minor – remember that the key signature tells you that every B and every E is a flat.

2.15 Doubling and omitting notes

In order to lay out the notes of chords in the best way for voices or for different types of instrument, it is often necessary to omit a note of a chord (usually the 5th) and/or to **double** a note.

Doubling means using the same pitch in more than one part – either exactly the same pitch (unison) or the same pitch but in a different octave.

Example 2.15 on the next page contains a short passage in three parts (that is, with three simultaneous melodic lines). Chord 3 is a complete triad, but some of the other chords include doubled notes, which means that one or more notes in the chord have to be omitted.

Look at chord 1 in the example. It has two Cs and an E – this is perfectly satisfactory since we still hear it as a C major chord, despite there being no G. Chord 14 has a G in all three parts. In the context this still implies a chord of G major, despite the absence of both B and D. We can say that chord 14 *implies* (rather than actually states) a triad of G major. Similarly, chord 1 implies, rather than states, a triad of C major.

Ex. 2.15   Purcell: *Dido and Aeneas* (adapted)

The following table identifies the first seven chords in this music, and shows which have doubled and omitted notes.

Number	Chord and position	Doublings and omissions
1	C root position	root (C) doubled, 5th (G) omitted
2	Am first inversion	3rd (C) doubled, 5th (E) omitted
3	G root position	
4	G root position	root (G) doubled, 5th (D) omitted
5	C root position	
6	Am root position	root (A) doubled, 5th (E) omitted
7	D root position	

Activity 2.15

Write a table similar to the one above to identify the triads, inversions, doublings and omitted notes in chords 8–14 of the music at the top of this page.

2.16 Doubling notes in four-part writing

A great deal of music is written in four parts, including chorales harmonised by Bach, much other music for choirs, and quartets of various kinds. Even some orchestral writing is basically in four parts, with various instruments doubling some or all of these basic four parts.

In four-part music, one note of a triad has to be doubled to make the fourth note. For instance, you might have C C G E rather than C E G, as shown in Example 2.16.

Ex. 2.16

As we noted previously, the parts which create the doubling may play or sing in unison or may be one, two or more octaves apart.

There is some choice in which note is best to double, but for the present, let's keep it simple – just remember that:

- In $\frac{5}{3}$ chords, the root is most commonly doubled
- In $\frac{6}{3}$ chords, there is greater variety (but composers avoid doubling note 7 of the scale, the leading note)
- In $\frac{6}{4}$ chords, the 5th (which is also the bass note) is usually doubled.

7th chords have four notes and therefore doubling is not always necessary in four-part writing. However, composers sometimes omit the 5th of 7th chords in root position, and double the root. Inversions of 7th chords rarely involve doubling or omitting notes.

Activity 2.16

Study the following excerpt from a piano piece by Schumann. The key is G major and the music is in four parts. Even where there are only three notes, as in the first chord, Schumann thinks in terms of two parts in the right hand and two in the left, which is why there are two stems on the note in the left hand.

Schumann: *Choral* (adapted)

vi

a Below the bass stave, label each chord with a Roman numeral and, if necessary, a letter to show its inversion. The first answer is given.

b Show which note of each chord has been doubled by writing R, 3rd or 5th above the treble stave. There are two chords without doubled notes. Why is this?

2.17 Additional harmony notes

In two-part music, triads and 7th chords can only ever be implied, because at least one note is always omitted.

However, you can sometimes give an impression of fuller harmony by using two or more different notes from the same chord in succession in one part, against a single note in another part. These extra notes are called **additional harmony notes**, and they are marked * in Example 2.17. They are useful in all kinds of music, however many parts there are.

Corelli: Violin Sonata, Op. 5 No. 7

Ex. 2.17

D minor: i   vii   i   ib   V   i

Activity 2.17

The following passage is in F major. Write the correct chord symbol at each of the places marked * and draw a circle round all additional harmony notes.

Mozart: *Menuett* K. 2 (adapted)

3 Chord progressions

3.1 What are chord progressions?

Any two or more chords heard in succession can be called a harmonic progression but the term **chord progression** is often used to describe particular successions of chords that have become regular, even standard, parts of our harmonic vocabulary.

Knowing about chord progressions will help you

- Analyse music (see especially Chapter 6)
- Choose chords when harmonising melodies (see Chapter 7)
- Prepare for the skills needed in the next book, *A Level Music Harmony Workbook 2*
- Compose music
- Understand better the pieces you play or sing.

3.2 Functional harmony

From the late 17th century until well into the 19th century (and in much later music as well) harmony was **functional** – that is, an important function or purpose of the chord progressions used was to establish and maintain a key.

> Be careful with centuries! The 17th century included the years 1600 to 1699 (or some would say 1601 to 1700). So 1850 is in the middle of the 19th century.

Before seeing in detail how chord progressions work, we need to divide individual chords into three main groups according to their functions:

- **The tonic group**: chord I and occasional alternatives, notably VI. Chord I has the tonic of the scale as its root, and is normally the only chord considered stable enough for a whole piece to end on.

- **The dominant group**: chord V, chord V^7, and chord VII (usually in first inversion, as VIIb). The close relationship between these three chords is shown in Example 3.2. They all contain note 7, which has a powerful tendency to rise to 8, hence the name 'leading note'. It quite literally leads back to the upper tonic and so to the tonic group of chords.

Ex. 3.2
C major

V V^7 vii

C major

ii ii^7 IV

- **The subdominant group**: the subdominant chord IV, plus chords II and II^7. The close relationship between these three chords is also shown in Example 3.2.

3.3 Chords I and V

Chords I and V (or V^7) are the two chords best able to establish and maintain a key, and much music (particularly in the 18th century) makes extensive use of them. Composers often move from I to $V^{(7)}$ (including their inversions) and from $V^{(7)}$ to I. This progression is not limited to 18th-century music, as you can see in this hit tune from the 1925 Broadway show, *No, No, Nanette:*

Ex. 3.3.1

Vincent Youmans: *I Want to be Happy*

I want to be hap-py, but I won't be hap-py

Till I make you hap-py too. _____

Here is the same progression from a piece written by Mozart some 150 years earlier. The key is
B♭ major and the chords are inverted, but the harmonic progression is otherwise identical.

Ex. 3.3.2   Mozart: Minuet from Piano Sonata K. 282

B♭ major: Ib ⟶ V⁷d   V⁷d ⟶ Ib

Play this example and notice the way in which the first phrase (marked with a bracket) is
followed by a second phrase (also bracketed) of the same length. This aurally satisfying type
of construction is often called a **question and answer**.

In Example 3.3.2 the first phrase sounds questioning because it invites more – it ends with
the leading note in the melody, supported by (an incomplete) chord of V⁷d, both sounding
unfinished. The second phrase sounds like an answer, because the harmony resolves onto the
tonic chord (Ib) and the melody returns to the tonic note. The two phrases are united by their
identical length and, in this case, their identical rhythm.

It is often useful to think of chords I and V⁽⁷⁾ as 'home and away' – chord I invites a journey
away, while chord V⁽⁷⁾ signals a need to return home.

3.4 The progression V–I

Chords V–I *in that order* make the strongest of all progressions – strong enough even to bring
an entire section or piece to a convincing end.

The progression V–I includes movement from the leading note (7) in chord V to the upper
tonic (8) in chord I. The leading note has a strong urge to move to the tonic. Try singing or
playing a scale and stopping on note 7!

Example 3.4.1 shows a phrase from a major-key hymn tune in which chords V–I are used
twice. If it helps, play just the outer parts, soprano and bass. Example 3.4.2 is an extract
from a chorus by Purcell. Chords V–I appear three times in C minor and then twice in E♭,
the relative major.

S S Wesley: *Almsgiving*

Ex. 3.4.1

E major: V ⟶ I   V ⟶ I

Ex. 3.4.2   Purcell: *Dido and Aeneas*

C minor: V ⟶ I   V ⟶ I   V ⟶ I
                              E♭ major: V⟶I   V ⟶ I

Activity 3.4

Mark examples of the progression V–I in the following extract.

William Croft (attributed): *Hanover* (adapted)

G major: iib

3.5 Perfect cadences

Both musical examples in **Section 3.4** finish with the progression V–I. The two chords that end a phrase are known as a **cadence**. The 'approach chord(s)' immediately before the cadence itself are often regarded as part of the complete cadential progression.

The V–I cadence is a **perfect cadence**. In functional harmony it is by far the most widely-used type of cadence.

The adjective 'perfect' comes from a Latin word meaning finished or complete, but in practice not all perfect cadences are equally final. It depends partly on how final-sounding the melody is. If the tune ends with notes 2–1 or 7–8, the effect is likely to be more final than with, for example, 5–3.

The bass in a perfect cadence can either descend from note 5 to note 1, as it does at the end of Example 3.4.2, or it can rise from note 5 to note 8 (the upper tonic) as it does at the end of Example 3.4.1. The descent of the bass from V to I, beneath a melody that ascends from note 7 to note 8, provides the most definitive type of perfect cadence, especially if the first chord is V^7 rather than just V:

Ex. 3.5

C major: V^7 I

Chord *viib* sometimes substitutes for V$^{(7)}$ in perfect cadences, although the effect is not as strong: for an example, see the chord marked * in **Activity 3.17 (a)** on page 46.

Activity 3.5

Look for, and listen to, more examples of perfect cadences. Look (for instance) at Chapter 6, and at more or less any 18th-century music.

3.6 Approaching a perfect cadence

Look at the perfect cadence in bars 3–4 of **Activity 3.4** at the top of this page. It is preceded by chord iib, which is one of the subdominant group of chords. In fact, any of the chords from that group makes an effective approach to a perfect cadence.

Many phrases that conclude with a perfect cadence end with the following three chords:

- A chord from the subdominant group, then
- A chord from the dominant group (usually V or V^7), and finally
- Chord I from the tonic group.

Here are two more examples, one in A minor and the other in G major:

Ex. 3.6.1 — Mendelssohn: *Elijah*

As we have heard with our ears.

A minor: iv⁷ → V⁷ → i

Ex. 3.6.2 — Scottish traditional

For the sake of auld lang syne.

G major: IV → V → I

Activity 3.6

Here are the final phrases from four Christmas carols, all ending on the tonic. Name the key of each and add chord symbols at the places marked *, choosing an approach chord from the subdominant group followed by a perfect cadence in every case.

Traditional: *We Wish You a Merry Christmas*

*   *   *

Este's Psalter: *While Shepherds Watched*

*   *   *

W J Kirkpatrick: *Away in a Manger*

*   *   *

Traditional: *O Little Town of Bethlehem*

*   *   *

3.7 The cadential $^6_4$

The perfect cadence can also be approached from chord Ic. Although this is a very common approach, Ic is not really a fully independent chord but more a decoration of chord V, with which it shares the same bass note. For that reason, Ic is often used between an approach chord from the subdominant group and the actual perfect cadence, in such patterns as IV–Ic–V⁽⁷⁾–I:

Traditional spiritual melody: *We Shall Overcome*

We shall ov – er – come some day.

Ex. 3.7

C major: IV Ic V⁷ I

In Example 3.7, notice how:

- E in chord Ic moves down by step to D in chord V
- C in chord Ic moves down by step to B in chord V
- Both chords have G in the bass.

In terms of intervals above the bass, we hear a 6th falling to a 5th, and a 4th falling to a 3rd. This $^6_4 – ^5_3$ movement is the essence of the Ic–V progression. When chord Ic is used in this cadential position it is often called the **cadential $^6_4$**.

Activity 3.7

Add notes on the treble stave of these two passages to complete chords Ic and V in the places indicated. Each chord requires two more notes. Check that the notes in each of your $\frac{6}{4}$ chords fall by step to the following $\frac{5}{3}$ chord, then play both phrases.

Marcello: Keyboard Sonata No. 2

G major: vi iib Ic V I

Traditional spiritual

I ain't gon-na stu-dy war no more.

F major: Ib ii Ic V I

3.8 Interrupted cadences

If you replace chord I in a perfect cadence with some other chord, you create an **interrupted cadence** – so called because it interrupts the expected progress of the music to the tonic. It is sometime used as a 'delaying tactic', creating the expectation that a perfect cadence will soon follow, as in Example 3.8.

Ex. 3.8

Handel: *Water Music* (adapted)

G major: iib → Ic → V^7 → vi

Interrupted

iib → Ic → V^7 → I

Perfect

Interrupted cadences frequently end with chord VI, as here, but any chord that creates an effective surprise (for example IVb) is possible. In a minor key, chord VI is major, which makes the effect of an interrupted cadence more arresting. Mozart's Requiem (a large-scale work for singers and orchestra) ends with the magnificent effect of a diminished 7th used as the second chord of an interrupted cadence – but after a silence, the expected perfect cadence follows to conclude the work.

Chord VI cannot replace I at a final cadence and it doesn't usually replace the tonic chord at the start of a piece either, because it is not very helpful in establishing the key. Whether or not VI is a suitable alternative to I in mid phrase will depend on the context. In general, remember that interruputed cadences are *far* less common than perfect cadences.

Activity 3.8

a Here is the ending of a well-known piece, with the last chord missing. Label the three printed chords and then play the passage with a tonic chord at the end, to make a perfect cadence. Then try ending on chord vi to create an interrupted cadence. Note the difference.

G major:

Next, see if you can play the passage in *G minor*, still with an interrupted cadence (the final chord should be E♭ major).

Finally try ending on a diminished 7th, for a really surprising interruption!

b Name the key, label all the chords and identify both of the cadences indicated by brackets in these two final phrases from a well-known Christmas carol.

Franz Gruber: *Silent Night* (adapted)

3.9 Imperfect cadences

The progression I–V can be used almost anywhere – at the beginning, in the middle, or at the end of a phrase. At the end of a phrase it forms an **imperfect cadence**.

Imperfect cadences sound far less final than perfect cadences – ending on chord V leaves the music open to continue, not least since chord V includes the leading note (note 7) that has not yet fulfilled its destiny of rising to note 8. The adjective 'imperfect' comes from a Latin word meaning incomplete.

Example 3.9.1 contains two I–V progressions, the second of which creates an imperfect cadence.

Ex. 3.9.1

W H Havergal: *Franconia*

D major: I ⟶ V   I ⟶ V

Imperfect cadences must end with chord V, but they need not have I as the first chord. For example, many imperfect cadences consist of the progression ii–V or variants such as iib–V and ii⁷b–V.

Chord V is often preceded by a cadential $^6_4$ (chord Ic) in imperfect cadences, just as it is in perfect cadences, particularly in music of the Classical period:

Ex. 3.9.2

Haydn: *The Creation*

C major: ii ⟶ Ic ⟶ V

Activity 3.9

Play each of the following. In each case identify the key and the chords marked *, and identify the cadences formed by these chords.

Mildred J. Hill: *Happy Birthday to You!*

Mozart: *The Magic Flute*

Corelli: Trio Sonata, Op. 2 No. 4

3.10 Plagal cadences

The subdominant chord (IV) is widely used before and after I. Chords IV–I, when used at the end of phrase, make a **plagal cadence**.

A plagal cadence, like a perfect cadence, can end a section or piece, because its final chord is I, although it is used *far* less frequently than the perfect cadence.

Years ago it was common in church to sing 'Amen' to a plagal cadence at the end of a hymn and for this reason, people still occasionally call it an 'Amen' cadence.

Ex. 3.10

A major: IV   I

3.11 Cadence summary

Here is a summary of the four cadences we have studied. Remember that perfect and imperfect cadences are used far more frequently than the other two types.

- Perfect: $V^{(7)}$ to I
- Imperfect: any chord to V (such as $iib^{(7)}$ –V)
- Interrupted: $V^{(7)}$ to any chord except I (often $V^{(7)}$ –vi)
- Plagal: IV to I.

Activity 3.11

Study this hymn and then:

(i) Name the keys in the three places indicated

(ii) Identify each of the cadences marked with a bracket

(iii) Label the approach chords marked *.

Remember to think in terms of the new key in bars 9–12.

Melody by H J Gauntlett: *Laudate Dominum*

Key?

Key? * * Key? * *

3.12 The circle of 5ths

Movement from V to I is so strong largely because of the downward leap of a 5th between the roots of the two chords. Other progressions with roots that fall a 5th (including I–IV) possess something of the same strength.

In practice 'down a 5th' can also mean 'up a 4th', since exactly the same pitches are involved. Look back at the V– I progressions you found in **Activity 3.4** (page 36) – in the first and third, the bass rises from D to G, while in the second it falls from D to the G below, and yet the chord progressions are all V–I.

If you start on chord I and keep moving down in 5ths or up in 4ths, you will eventually return to the tonic chord and have an important and useful chord progression called the **circle of 5ths**. Ascending 4ths usually alternate with descending 5ths in a circle of 5ths so that the bass part doesn't descend into an impossibly low region:

Ex. 3.12.1

C	F	B dim	Em	Am	Dm	G	C
I	IV	*vii*	iii	vi	ii	V	I

Notice that the interval between the second and third roots in this example is an augmented 4th (it would be a diminished 5th if the bass fell from F to the B below). While it is possible to move only in perfect 4ths and perfect 5ths it would take twelve moves to come full circle rather than seven and is something almost never done.

Even the seven-chord circle of 5ths is not often used in full, although here in outline is an example from a 1954 hit made famous by Frank Sinatra. Notice that this time the circle begins and ends on a chord of A minor.

Ex. 3.12.2   Bart Howard: *Fly Me to the Moon* (adapted)

Fly me to the moon and let me play a - mong the stars,

Am   Dm⁷   G   C

Let me see what spring is like on Ju - pi - ter and Mars.

F   B dim⁷   E   Am

This example, like a few later ones in the chapter, includes some notes in the tune that are not in the underlying chords. We will learn about these in the next chapter, but for now just be aware that they don't alter the basic harmony.

More typically, composers tend to use smaller segments from the circle of 5ths, such as the chord progression vi–ii–V–I. You can see an example in bars 3–4[1] of the music at the top of page 36 (chord ii is inverted here to provide a smoother bass part).

References such as bar 4[1] mean bar 4, beat 1.

3.13 Harmonic sequences

Look at Example 3.12.2 and compare bars 5–8 with the first four bars. Do you see that the tune is similar, except that it is two notes lower? This is known as a **melodic sequence**.

The chords also follow a similar pattern – the pattern of roots descending by 5ths and rising by 4ths in bars 1–4 is repeated in bars 5–8, but two notes lower. A chord progression repeated at a different pitch is called an **harmonic sequence**, and will usually accompany a melodic sequence, as it does here.

Circles of 5ths usually generate harmonic sequences of this kind, but it is also possible to create them with other chord progressions. In Example 3.13 the sequences are formed from repeated pairs of chords with roots that fall a 4th. Each repetition of the pattern is a 3rd lower than the previous one, giving the progression:

- I–V–I–V, vi–iii–vi–iii, IV–I–IV–I.

Ex. 3.13   Handel: *Alexander's Feast*

Sa - cred to love,   sa - cred to love,   sa - cred to har - mo - ny,   sa - cred to love.

F major: I   V   I   V   vi   iii   vi   iii   IV   I   IV   I

Notice the appearance of chord iii in Example 3.13 – we haven't often encountered this rather rare triad before. It is often followed by chord vi or chord IV, as it is here. Look at bars 5[3]–6[1] of the music for **Activity 3.11** on page 40 and you will see iiib followed by IV (Bm/D – C in the key of G major).

Activity 3.13

a In the example below, the melody consists of **broken chords**. That is, the notes of each chord are played individually in various patterns, sometimes leaping down by more than an octave to prevent the patterns becoming too predictable. This doesn't affect the harmony, though – just add together the notes of each broken chord to work out what it is, as shown right.

= B♭ major

Label the chords in the following music, and show where the harmonic sequences occur by marking each one with a bracket.

Handel: Violin Sonata No. 3

b Write in the three missing chords in this circle of 5ths in the key of D major:

D – G – C♯ dim – F♯m – _____ – Em – _____ – _____

3.14 Other effective chord progressions

In addition to chords whose roots fall in 5ths, the following progressions work well and are very useful:

- **Roots that rise by a 5th** (or fall by a 4th), such as IV–I
- **Roots that rise by a 2nd**, such as V–VI and I–II
- **Roots that fall by a 3rd**, such as I down to VI, VI–IV, and IV–II. When strung together the first two of these progressions form the start of the chord pattern I–VI–IV–V, a favourite of generations of would-be pianists:

Ex. 3.14

C major: I   vi   IV   V

This is sometimes called the 'doo-wop' progression, because of its frequent use in the style of 1950s' pop known as doo-wop. A similar 'falling 3rds' progression is I–VI–IV–II–V–I, often used in early rock and roll. Both tended to be over-used and can (like the circle of 5ths) sound something of a cliché. However, stock progressions such as these are a good way of learning about harmony, especially if you try improvising around them in different keys.

We can summarise all of our work on progressions with the following rule of thumb: good progressions to lead up to a cadence can generally be formed from chords that have roots which go:

- **Up a 2nd, down a 3rd, up a 4th or down a 5th.**

3.15 Pedals

When composers want to emphasise the tonic or the dominant while creating additional harmonic interest and variety, they often use a **pedal**. This is a long sustained note (or successive repetitions of the same note) with changing harmonies going on around it.

The most common type is a **dominant pedal**. Typically it helps build a sense of expectation that chord I will arrive as a piece nears its end. The majority of pedals are in the bass, but they can occur at the top of the texture (an **inverted pedal**), or in an inner part (an **inner pedal**). In fact, Sullivan uses all three types in Example 3.15.1, although the inverted and inner pedals (also on G) have been omitted for clarity. This section of so-called 'dominant preparation' lasts for 19 bars in all, before one of the big tunes of the operetta returns in a triumphantly **ff** C major.

Ex. 3.15.1   Sullivan: *The Pirates of Penzance* (Overture)

A **tonic pedal** may be used at the beginning of a movement to help establish the key, as in Example 3.15.2, or at the end, to help bring a piece to a satisfying and often peaceful conclusion.

Ex. 3.15.2   Bach: Prelude in C, BWV 939

C major: I   (I$^{\flat 7}$)   IV   V   (V^7)   I

When using a pedal, the surrounding harmony needs to form proper harmonic progressions, just as it would if the pedal wasn't there. As you can see above, the chords are identified just as they would be if there was no pedal.

3.16 Modulation

Modulation is the process of changing key. Changes of key provide welcome variety, and are valuable in terms of form and structure. Most pieces of any length move away from their starting key (the tonic) to one or more other keys and then return to the tonic before the end, as we saw in the music for **Activity 3.11** on pages 40-41.

Related keys

Modulations are most commonly to **related keys** – that is, to keys with the same signature as the tonic key, or with one more, or one fewer, sharps or flats. You may also encounter modulations between tonic minor and tonic major keys, for example from C minor to C major, or vice versa.

The following table shows these relationships for a piece in D major. In practice, most major-key works in the Baroque and Classical periods will modulate to the **dominant** at some point. Modulations to other related keys may or may not occur.

Subdominant   Tonic   **Dominant**

G major: V^7 I   D major: V^7 I   A major: V^7 I

Relative minor of   Relative minor   Relative minor
the subdominant   of the dominant

E minor: V^7 i   B minor: V^7 i   F♯ minor: V^7 i

Tonic minor

D minor: V^7 i

Chords V^7 and I are shown in each key because these two chords are the main means by which a key is established.

Notice in the example above that:

- The relative minor has the same key signature as its relative major, but you need to sharpen note 7 in the minor key

- The dominant has one sharp *more* than the tonic, and you also need to sharpen note 7 in the relative minor of the dominant

- The subdominant has one sharp *fewer* than the tonic, but you also need to sharpen note 7 in the relative minor of the subdominant.

The same principles hold good for all keys. When you have no more sharps to take away you are in C major or A minor. After that you need to add flats to keep going in a subdominant direction.

Here is a table of keys related to a minor key, using B minor as the example. In minor keys, a structurally-important modulation to the **relative major** is highly likely.

The tables above remind you of the key signatures for the various related keys. However, in practice there is not normally a change of key signature when music modulates (except occasionally for the change between tonic minor and tonic major).

Instead, you must use accidentals to represent the notes of the new key. This includes adding sharps or flats before individual notes to supplement those in the key signature, and/or adding naturals before individual notes to cancel sharps or flats present in the key signature.

This process needs great care, as it is easy to miss vital accidentals. You may find it helps to write out the note names of the new scale when music modulates.

3.17 How modulation works

The strongest of all chord progressions is V⁷–I. Unlike a pair of chords such as Am and C, which can occur in several different keys, V⁷–I can only ever occur in one key (the tonic). Consider G⁷–C.

This progression defines the key of C major because:

- It contains F♮ so it cannot belong to a key with any sharps

- It contains B♮ so it cannot belong to a key with any flats

- It contains G♮ so it cannot belong to A minor, the only other key with no sharps or flats in its key signature.

The same logic holds good for V⁷–I in any key, major or minor, making it the most decisive way to create a modulation and establish a new key.

In Example 3.17.1 below:

- Phrase 1 stays in F major and ends with an interrupted cadence in that key

- Phrase 2 stays in F major and ends with an imperfect cadence in that key

- Phrase 3 modulates to the dominant key, which is confirmed by the definitive perfect cadence V⁷–I in C major (G⁷–C) at the end of this phrase

■ Phrase 4 modulates back to the tonic key, which is confirmed by the definitive perfect cadence V^7–I in F major (C^7–F) at the end of this final phrase.

If the music modulates there will usually be a second modulation in order to return to the tonic key before the end (except in the case of short extracts used as examples, such as those below). Even if there are modulations to several different keys in succession you should still normally expect the music to modulate back to the tonic for the final phrase(s) of the passage.

Ex. 3.17.1

Henry Jenner: *Quam dilecta*

The chord marked * is Vb in F major, the key we are leaving, and Ib in C major, the key that is about to be established by the cadence at the end of phrase 3.

A chord that exists both in the old key and the new is called a **pivot chord** and it produces a particularly smooth transition to the new key. The same chord is used as a pivot back to F major at the start of phrase 4.

A pivot chord is not essential, but omitting it and plunging straight into a dominant 7th in the new key produces a much more abrupt modulation:

Ex. 3.17.2

Beethoven: Piano Sonata in E♭, Op. 81a

Activity 3.17

a Identify the three keys in the following passage by Handel:

Handel: *Acis and Galatea*

Notice the chord marked * in the final cadence of this passage. It is chord *viib* and is used as a substitute for $V^{(7)}$ in this perfect cadence.

b In the above passage, write Ic below the example of a cadential $\frac{6}{4}$.

c Study the modulation in the following passage, which includes a pivot chord indicated by a shaded box, and then complete the sentences below.

Bach: Minuet from French Suite No. 3, BWV 814

This passage begins in the key of _____ and ends in the key of _____ .

The pivot chord is chord _____ in the starting key, and chord _____

in the final key of the passage.

d The progression shown right ends with an imperfect cadence.
Add an accidental to make the chords modulate to the dominant
instead.

3.18 Secondary dominants

Compare the following progressions:

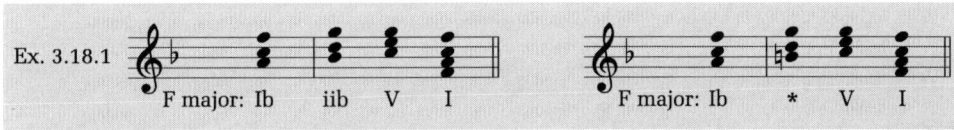

The second is the same as the first, apart from the chord marked *. The B♮ in this cadence
approach chord seems to be starting a modulation to C major, but this is immediately nullified
in favour of a perfect cadence in F major. So in fact there is no modulation – the approach
chord in the second progression is a type of chromatic chord (that is, one outside of the
current key) known as a **secondary dominant**.

A secondary dominant is the *major* chord whose root is a perfect 5th above any note of
the scale except the tonic (because that would be the normal dominant chord) – although
secondary dominants above the leading note are not used since they would be too remote
from the current key.

The chord marked * in Example 3.18.1 is the first inversion of G major.
This G major triad acts as a temporary 'dominant' to the chord of C that
follows it, as shown in Example 3.18.2. Note that there is **no modulation**
because the cadence itself asserts the key of F major.

Ex. 3.18.2

V of V V I

Here are the secondary dominants in the key of C major – they often include
a minor 7th above the root, as shown in this example:

Ex. 3.18.3

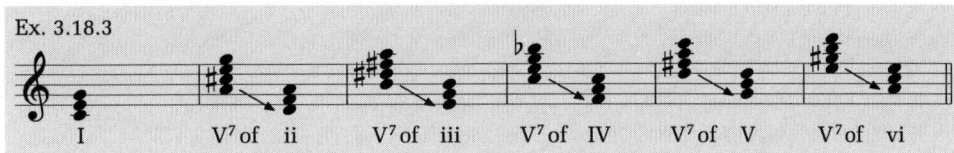

The essence of these progressions is again the strength of the falling 5th from the root of the
chromatic chord to the root of the chord that follows. Instead of changing key, they serve to
reinforce the importance of the chord onto which they fall.

In the next two examples, the secondary dominants are marked * (they all include 7ths above the root):

Ex. 3.18.4 — Johnny Marks: *Rudolph the Red-Nosed Reindeer*

Secondary dominants are frequently used in first inversion (or in third inversion if they include a 7th above the root), as in the next example, in which the underlying harmonic progression is shown in small notes below the main stave:

Ex. 3.18.5 — Mozart: Piano Sonata in G, K. 283

Look again at Examples 3.18.4 and 3.18.5 above and see if you can spot an old friend. It is the circle of 5ths, but with more major chords than before: E^7–A^7–D^7–G^7–C. As these two examples show, the falling-5ths progression can be found in music of very different times and styles.

A note about accidentals

Because secondary dominants are chromatic they always involve the use of accidentals, and so this is a good moment to review the various different purposes for which accidentals are needed.

They may be:

- The raised or lowered versions of notes 6 and 7 in a minor key
- Chromatic alterations, such as those needed in secondary-dominant chords
- Pitches needed for a new key because of a modulation.

In other words, an accidental doesn't always mean a modulation. In fact, modulation from a minor key to its relative major can even occur without any accidental at all, as it is often possible just to stop sharpening the minor key's leading note – as when C♯ becomes plain C in bars 2 and 3 of Example 4.4 on page 54. Remember, it is the presence of a definitive cadence that really confirms the key of the music.

Activity 3.18

a Identify the two secondary-dominant chords in the following passage and describe the function of each (e.g. V7 of iii).

James Molloy: *Love's Old Sweet Song*

b Name the final cadence in this extract.

c Does the music above modulate?

d Name the harmonic progression used in bars 5–8 of the passage.

e Change the chords marked * below into secondary dominants by adding the appropriate accidentals.

Haydn: *The Seasons*

C major   *

Mozart: *The Magic Flute*

B♭ major   *

Purcell: *The Fairy Queen*

B minor   *   *

3.19 The tierce de Picardie

Play the following passage:

Mundy: *Ah, Helpless Wretch*

Ex 3.19

G minor   V ⟶ I♮3

Although the key is G minor, the final tonic chord is G *major*. When a major version of chord I is used to brighten the ending of a passage in a minor key it is known as a **tierce de Picardie**. The origin of the term is unclear, but 'tierce' refers to the 3rd of the tonic chord (which is unexpectedly major) and it seems likely that this practice was associated in bygone times with music from the region of Picardy in France.

Example 3.19 was composed in about 1585, at a time when composers were reluctant to end significant sections of a piece on a minor chord. Instead, 16th- and 17th-century composers usually preferred to end a minor-key passage with bare octaves or a bare 5th (as in the Purcell example from part **e** of **Activity 3.18** above) – or else they would use a tierce de Picardie in order to end on a major chord.

The tierce de Picardie thus occurs as the final chord of perfect and plagal cadences in many Renaissance and early Baroque pieces and is not regarded as a type of modulation. By the late 18th century the use of this device had become rare, as composers increasingly accepted the slightly sour effect of actually ending on a minor chord.

Activity 3.19

Name the key of each of the following passages, label the chords and then add an accidental to create a tierce de Picardie at the end of each.

3.20 Harmonic rhythm

As you worked through the music in this chapter you may have noticed that in the more hymn-like examples (such as those above) the chords change on almost every note, while in others (such as the song in **Activity 3.18 (a)**), the chords change once a bar or less.

The rate at which chords change is known as the **harmonic rhythm** and is an important element in the style of different types of music. It is something that we will return to later in the book.

4 Part-writing and non-chord notes

4.1 Definition of part-writing

Part-writing concerns the correct and stylish movement of individual parts within the chosen harmonies. In other words, part-writing is not about how you choose chords, but how you make best use of them when writing parts for instruments or voices. 'Voice-leading' is an alternative term for part-writing.

4.2 Tips for effective part-writing

Example 4.2.1 shows the progression vi–ii–V in C major. If this was allocated to three voices or instruments as it stands, the three parts would jump around in a disjointed way and would have no independence because they all move in **similar motion**, as shown by the staves on the right:

Ex. 4.2.1

Compare this with the layout of the same three chords shown in Example 4.2.2 below. Here, the lowest of the three parts – the 'bass' of the harmony– still contains leaps (**disjunct** movement) but the upper parts move much more smoothly because they use either stepwise (**conjunct**) movement or melodic intervals no larger than a 3rd.

Also, the highest part gains independence from the bass by moving in **contrary motion** – when the bass goes down, it goes up, and vice versa. All of this has been achieved simply by using an open spacing for the second of the three chords.

Ex. 4.2.2

One of the secrets of good part-writing is to avoid large leaps, especially in the upper parts. You can avoid them by **adjusting chord spacing and note-doubling** – and perhaps by choosing an inverted chord rather than one in root position – in order to maximise the amount of stepwise movement.

It is not always possible to avoid large leaps in a melody or bass, but it is often best if the note after such a leap returns within the span of the interval:

Ex. 4.2.3

When laying out parts, remember the following points:

- Large leaps occasionally occur in melodies (and frequently in bass parts) but it is best to return within the interval whenever possible, as shown above.

- It is often good for inner parts to move as little as possible – frequently staying on the same note works well. Otherwise try to keep to conjunct movement and small leaps (especially 3rds).

- The frequent use of contrary motion between the melody and bass will help give these two most important parts a real sense of independent movement.

- A good texture can be achieved by keeping the upper parts fairly close together – in contrast, a sizeable gap (even of an octave or more) between the bass and the next part up will help give focus to the bass, and prevent it being muddied by other parts close by.

Names of voice parts

Four-part writing is often for voices, and the parts are named after the voices that sing them. The two-stave layout of Example 4.2.4 below is typical. The topmost part is the **soprano**, written with upward stems. The part with downward stems on the same stave is the **alto**. The part with upward stems on the second of the two staves is the **tenor**, and the part with downward stems on this stave is the **bass**.

Example 4.2.4 shows a passage of simple yet effective four-part writing. The middle parts, while straightforward, have some melodic character and are never awkward to sing. All but one of the chords is in root position, so there are inevitably some leaps in the bass, although never more than a perfect 5th in this example.

Ex. 4.2.4   Este's Psalms: *While Shepherds Watched* (adapted)

F major: I ⟶ V vi IV ⟶ I V I V vi⁷
C major: ii⁷ V⁷ I

The chords that form the basis of this passage are shown on the small stave at the bottom of this example. Carefully study the way in which they have been used to create upper parts that avoid jagged contours.

Every triad has a doubled root in the four-part version and the 5th is omitted in the final chord, resulting in the root (C) appearing in three of the four parts. The use of a first-inversion chord of C major (three chords before the end) helps to prevent too many leaps in the bass. The 5th has been omitted from chord ii⁷ (and the root of this chord is doubled) again to maximise the amount of conjunct movement.

Activity 4.2

Complete the missing alto and tenor parts in the following progressions, using the chords indicated.

In (i) keep the alto on the same note throughout and make sure that the tenor moves entirely by step.

In (ii) the alto should begin by repeating the same note and end with movements of a minor 2nd, and the tenor should not leap by more than a 3rd.

G major: I V⁷d Ib V I

G minor: i ivb ii⁷b V i

A useful tip

When starting out on exercises of this sort, many people find it helpful to write down the notes of the chords in root position on a mini-stave, as shown below. Make sure you take account of sharps or flats in the key signature and in minor keys be certain to include the necessary accidental for the raised leading-note.

You should make similar mini-staves for yourself when working on later exercises, until you really feel confident in knowing the chords for the key concerned.

4.3 Parallel perfect 5ths and octaves

The person who wrote Example 4.3.1 has done two things which are unwise:

- Doubling the 5th in chord V without any good reason (normally the root should be doubled whenever possible)
- Letting the tenor leap a 4th when it could have repeated the D in the first chord.

As a result the tenor and bass move in **parallel perfect 5ths**, often referred to as **consecutive 5ths**. In traditional harmony there is a ban on parallel perfect 5ths in any given pair of parts, as well as on **parallel octaves** and **parallel unisons**. This is because these particular consecutive intervals rob the parts involved of their individuality.

You need to be aware that there has to be some movement before consecutives are caused – simply repeating a 5th, as in Example 4.3.2, is fine.

You should also realise that we are referring only to the basic parts in traditional harmony. It is common to double a melody or bass in octaves for a complete phrase (or longer) in many other types of music (as in the piano extract shown in Example 4.4). And in less traditional harmony, composers such as Debussy have made effective use of sonorities produced by parts moving in consecutive 5ths. But for the purpose of harmony exercises, consecutive 5ths, octaves and unisons must be avoided.

Ex. 4.3.1

G: I V

Ex. 4.3.2

F: I I

When checking for forbidden consecutives, you need to examine every combination of two parts. In four-part writing that means six checks:

- Soprano and alto
- Soprano and tenor
- Soprano and bass
- Alto and tenor
- Alto and bass
- Tenor and bass.

In the following example there are consecutive octaves between soprano and bass, and alto and bass, plus two sets of consecutive 5ths between other pairs of parts:

Ex. 4.3.3

Activity 4.3

Indicate consecutive 5ths and consecutive octaves in the following passages by drawing arrows between the notes concerned (as in Example 4.3.3 above). There are three forbidden consecutives in the first example and four in the second.

(i)

(ii)

4.4 Other types of movement

Occasional parallel 3rds or 6ths can be effective, but parallel 2nds and 7ths are not part of traditional harmonic styles. As we saw on page 51, contrary motion is preferable between soprano and bass, and makes it much easier to avoid forbidden consecutives between these parts. In the following example notice how Schumann's strong bass part in octaves moves mainly in contrary motion to the melody.

Ex. 4.4   Schumann: *Album for the Young*, No. 41

Oblique motion, in which one part stays on the same pitch while the other part moves up or down, is another good way of achieving independent soprano and bass parts, and of avoiding consecutives. An example of oblique motion is shown near the start of the music for **Activity 4.4** on the next page.

Activity 4.4

Between the staves in the following music, write '**C**' where there is contrary motion, '**S**' for similar motion, and '**O**' for oblique motion. The first two answers are given.

Sibelius: *Finlandia* (adapted)

4.5 Tendency notes

Good part-writing involves controlling the various parts, but the best results come when we work *with* the notes rather than trying to force them artificially.

In **Section 3.2** (on page 34) we noted that the leading note (note 7 of the scale) has a strong tendency to rise to the tonic. Other notes also have strong tendencies to move in certain directions – particularly notes that do not belong to the chord currently in use and the dissonant 7th in 7th chords. We shall find out more about these now.

4.6 An introduction to non-chord notes and dissonance

To make music more interesting, composers often include notes that are not part of the current chord. For example, we might briefly hear a D in one part while other parts are sounding a C major chord. These additional notes help to provide rhythmic movement and a better sense of melodic flow, and may be termed **non-chord notes**. Some people call them **unessential notes** because they are not essential to the basic harmony, but this risks undervaluing the vital effect they have.

To see how important non-chord notes are to so much music, play the whole of the following example. Version (i) shows the chords in a two-part layout. Version (ii) fills many of the gaps between notes in the melody of the first version, showing how the basic harmonies support a well-known tune:

Ex. 4.6 (i)

Ex. 4.6 (ii)

Traditional (arranged Grainger): *Country Gardens* (adapted)

4.7 Passing notes

The most common type of non-chord note is the **passing note**. Where there is a leap of a 3rd a passing note can be inserted to fill in the gap with stepwise movement and so add rhythmic life and movement. Never forget: **a passing note must always be approached and quitted by step in the same direction**, which can be up or down.

Unaccented passing notes

Look back at Example 4.6 (ii). The semiquavers are all passing notes. To be more precise, they are all **unaccented passing notes** – that is, they don't come on the beat, they just fill the gaps between chord notes. Most passing notes are unaccented and half a beat in length, like the one marked * in Example 4.7.1 – those in Example 4.6 are only semiquavers because the tune is particularly jaunty.

Ex. 4.7.1

C: iii   vi

Here are some more points about unaccented passing notes (letters in brackets refer to the illustrations in Example 4.7.2 below):

- A passing note may lie between two notes from the same chord (a), or two notes belonging to different chords (b).

- Two passing notes may be used at the same time, making parallel 3rds (c) or, less often, parallel 6ths. Or they may move in contrary motion, usually with a 10th moving to a 6th via an octave or vice versa, as shown in (d). Very occasionally three passing notes are used at once.

- **Passing notes can cause consecutives** (e) where there would not have been any before (f).

- Passing notes may occur in any part, but too many can sound fussy.

- Passing notes are usually **diatonic** (that is, they use notes from the current key, like those below), although chromatic passing notes are possible.

Ex. 4.7.2 (a) (b) (c) (d) (e) (f)

Accented passing notes

Accented passing notes come *on* the beat, and are therefore rhythmically stronger than the harmony notes on either side. Like the unaccented type, they fill the gap between two harmony notes and provide additional rhythmic interest, but we hear more clearly the harmonic conflict between the non-chord note that creates the accented passing note and the underlying chord.

This conflict is known as **dissonance** and, used in a controlled way through stepwise movement, can spice up music, rather like adding pepper to make a meal tastier. The chord progression in Example 4.7.3 (a) is repeated at (b) with accented passing notes in the melody. They are printed in grey to reveal the underlying chords.

Ex. 4.7.3 (a)   Ex. 4.7.3 (b)

Activity 4.7

a Write 'PN' over each (unaccented) passing note in the melody of the following dance, and 'APN' above each accented passing note.

Haydn: Minuet, Hob. IX:3, No. 12 (adapted)

D major: I   iib   V   V⁷d

Ib   I   A major: *viib*   Ib   vi   V   I

When you have finished, check that each remaining unmarked note in the melody is a harmony note that belongs to the current chord.

b Add unaccented passing notes to *both parts* in the following passage to provide additional semiquaver movement. The key is E minor and so, if you choose to add passing notes at any of the places marked *, you will have to consider whether it is better to use the normal version of note 6 (C) or the raised version (C♯).

Senaillé: Sonata in E minor (adapted)

A suggestion for the first complete bar is printed on the small stave above the music, but you don't have to follow this unless you wish. Be careful not to overload the piece with passing notes – it is not necessary to add them in every place where they might be possible.

4.8 Auxiliary notes

An **auxiliary note** lies a step above or below two harmony notes of **the same pitch**. Auxiliary notes work in the same way as passing notes, except that they return to their starting pitch instead of carrying on up or down the scale. Example 4.8.1 includes three auxiliary notes, two upper and one lower, marked *. All three are diatonic and are short in relation to the harmony notes preceding and following them.

Ex. 4.8.1

Scottish traditional melody:
The Skye Boat Song

The chromatic auxiliary notes (marked * below) in Sousa's march *The Liberty Bell* are an important feature of the piece. Play the following extract, and then see how ordinary the music sounds if you substitute G♮ for G♯ in bar 1 and F♮ for F♯ in bar 5.

Ex. 4.8.2   Sousa: *The Liberty Bell*

Activity 4.8

a Label each auxiliary note 'AUX' and each passing note 'PN' in the piece below.

b Write **X** beneath a secondary-dominant chord and **Y** beneath a cadential $^6_4$.

Franz Gruber: *Silent Night* (adapted)

4.9 Suspensions

People sometimes find suspensions quite difficult to understand. First, here is an explanation with a minimum of jargon.

A suspension happens:

- At a change of chord, when
- One part hangs on to a note from the old chord, creating a clash, after which
- The delayed part falls by step to a note of the new chord.

Example 4.9.1 (a) shows four chords in G major and (b) shows the same progression with a suspension in the tenor part, marked with an arrow. When soprano, alto and bass move to chord V on the last beat, the tenor is left behind. Its G is not part of the D major chord. The resulting clash is resolved when the tenor catches up by falling to F♯, a note that *is* part of the new chord of D major.

The suspended note in this example is shown tied to the previous note, but it could have been re-sounded, as shown in Example 4.9.2 (a), or written as a dotted note, as shown in Example 4.9.2 (b) below. These are both suspensions.

Note that **not every tied note is a suspension**. There is no suspension in Example 4.9.2 (c) above: the D in the alto remains a chord note, and so we hear no clash.

Here now is a second description of a suspension, which will introduce you to the necessary technical vocabulary.

A suspension happens in three stages:

- The **preparation**: the note that will cause the suspension is first heard as part of a normal chord, usually on a rhythmically weak beat.
- The **suspension** itself: the prepared note is held over (or repeated) as the other parts move to a different chord, creating a dissonance between the bass and the suspended note.
- The **resolution**: the suspended note falls by step to a note of the new chord in order to 'resolve' the dissonance. The resolution should be on a weaker beat or weaker part of a beat than the suspension itself.

Look again at the suspension marked by an arrow in Example 4.9.2 (a). By staying on G the tenor has temporarily replaced the 3rd of the D major chord – this 3rd only appears when G resolves to F♯. Most suspensions follow a similar pattern. The suspension temporarily replaces the 3rd or root of the chord with a note that is one step higher. The suspended note then falls by step to the expected note, as seen here.

In most cases, **the resolution should not also be sounded in any other part**, since this can create a rough-sounding dissonance, although we shall note an exception to this later. Suspensions can occur in any part, although they are least common in the bass.

Suspensions are classified according to the intervals between the suspended part and the bass at the moments of suspension and resolution. Three intervals are dissonant with the bass – 4ths, 7ths and 9ths.

These give us the three main types of suspension:

- **4–3**, in which the 3rd of a root-position chord is temporarily replaced by a 4th above the bass. This then drops to the 3rd, as in Example 4.9.3 (a) below.

- **7–6**, in which the root of a first-inversion chord is temporarily replaced by a 7th above the bass. This then drops to a 6th above the bass, as in Example 4.9.3 (b).

- **9–8**, in which the upper root of a root-position chord is temporarily replaced by a 9th above the root in the bass. This 9th then drops a note to the upper root, as in Example 4.9.3 (c). This is the one type of suspension in which the resolution will already be sounding, since the root occurs in both the bass part and the resolution.

In all three cases, remember that the intervals can be compound. For instance, a 4th may be a compound 4th (that is, an octave plus a 4th).

Ex. 4.9.3

IV   I⁴ ⁻ ³   vi   iib⁷ ⁻ ⁶   Vb   I⁹ ⁻ ⁸

Suspensions appear in many types of music, especially that of the Baroque period. Often in Renaissance and Baroque music dissonances underline words that express pain or sorrow, but more often they simply provide valuable additional rhythmic movement. They are also useful in creating pleasing contrasts between tension (dissonance) and release (resolution) in the music.

Example 4.9.4 is from a trio sonata by Corelli. The suspensions (indicated by arrows) come in quick succession, the resolution of one serving also as the preparation of the next. This produces a **chain of suspensions**.

Ex. 4.9.4   Corelli: Trio Sonata, Op. 3 No. 4

Largo

Violin 1

Violin 2

9 - 8   4 - 3   9-8 4-3 9-8 4-3   4 - 3

Cello

In this example, notice how:

- The dissonance sounds for only a quaver in most of the suspensions – but the first one lasts for a crotchet. To maintain rhythmic interest, Corelli makes the bass part start moving (with a passing note on E) before the suspension has resolved.

- One resolution (marked ⌐ * ⌐ above) is decorated with a lower auxiliary – a very common Baroque technique. While D and C♯ crotchets would have been perfectly satisfactory, the semiquaver 'twiddle' adds interest in this slow-moving texture.

Ex. 4.9.5

9 - 8
*

Another way to decorate a resolution is to leap to a different chord note between the suspension and its resolution, as shown by the note marked * in Example 4.9.5.

Activity 4.9

The music below shows the parts for two violins and cello in another trio sonata by Corelli. Notice that the second violin part on the middle stave is sometimes higher than the first violin part on the top stave. These are therefore called **crossing parts**.

a Identify each suspension in this passage by writing the letters **P** above the preparation, **S** above the suspended note and **R** above the resolution. Also show the type of suspension by writing 4–3, 7–6 or 9–8 below the suspended note and its resolution. The first answer has been done for you.

Corelli: Trio Sonata, Op. 4 No. 8 (adapted)

b Write ⌐*⌐ above a suspension in this passage that has a decorated resolution, and draw a circle around a tie that does **not** involve a suspension.

c Add the indicated suspensions to the passages below by completing the soprano part in (i) and the alto part in (ii). Each needs three crotchets – one for the preparation, one for the suspension and one for the resolution.

4.10 Appoggiaturas

An **appoggiatura** is rather like a suspension without any preparation. It consists of a dissonance followed by a resolution on a weaker beat. The word appoggiatura means 'leaning note', describing the way the dissonance leans onto its resolution.

In bar 3 of the following example there are four appoggiaturas, each marked *. The 4–3, 7–6 or 9–8 patterns above the bass remind us of suspensions, but appoggiaturas are not prepared as suspensions are. An appoggiatura is, in fact, usually approached by a leap (unlike an accented passing note, which is approached by a step).

Mozart: Piano Sonata in B♭, K. 333

The 'leaning' effect of an appoggiatura is often used as an expressive device in songs – as at the start of *Yesterday* by Lennon and McCartney or in this famous tune from the 1961 film,

Breakfast at Tiffany's (notice that the second appoggiatura is approached by step, but it is too prominent to be described as an accented passing note):

Ex. 4.10.2 — Henry Mancini: *Moon River*

Appoggiaturas sometimes resolve upwards, like the one marked * in the music for **Activity 4.10** below. In fact, this is a **chromatic appoggiatura** because C♯ is not part of the key of C minor. Most chromatic appoggiaturas tend to resolve upwards.

In the 18th century, an appoggiatura would often be written as a small note, like an ornament, thus making the resolution (the actual harmony note) clearer to see:

Ex. 4.10.3 — Haydn, Minuet, Hob. IX:8, No. 3 — Played as:

Activity 4.10

Write **X** above each diatonic appoggiatura in the following passage and * above each chromatic appoggiatura. The key is C minor and the first chromatic appoggiatura has been marked for you.

Mozart: Piano Sonata in C minor, K. 457

4.11 Anticipations

An **anticipation** is a weak-beat dissonance that does what it says – it anticipates the next harmony note by introducing it before the rest of the chord.

Anticipations are usually short and typically involve sounding note 1 in the melody immediately before chord I in a perfect cadence, as shown by the note marked * in Example 4.11.

Ex. 4.11

4.12 7th chords: built-in dissonance

The dissonances described so far all use notes foreign to the underlying harmony.
For example, you can remove a passing note and the basic harmony will be unchanged,

even though the music may sound less interesting. However, a dissonance (namely the 7th above the root) is an integral part of the harmony in 7th chords.

Revise **sections 2.11–2.13** if you are unsure about using 7th chords.

In traditional harmony, the 7th of a 7th chord, like all other dissonances, needs to be resolved. Example 4.12.1 below shows V⁷ resolving to I in the key of D major, including various possible spacings and inversions.

The descending stepwise resolution of the dissonant note (the 7th above the root) is indicated by a *downward* arrow in each case. Chord V⁷ also contains the leading note which, as you know, has a tendency to move up to the tonic. This is shown by an *upward* arrow in each progression.

Ex. 4.12.1

D major: V⁷   I   V⁷   I   V⁷b   I   V⁷c   I   V⁷d   Ib

The two tendency notes in V⁷ pull in opposite directions – the 7th above the root wants to fall while the leading note wants to rise. This gives a powerful harmonic thrust from V⁷ onto the following chord I – no wonder so many composers regularly prefer V⁷ to V in perfect cadences!

The 7th in chords such as ii⁷ and the diminished 7th has a similar tendency to fall by step. And if you use chromatic notes, be aware that raised notes have a tendency to continue up a step while lowered notes want to fall a step. The chord marked * in Example 4.12.2 is a secondary dominant (V⁷ of V). It contains a raised note that wants to move up and a 7th that wants to fall (both marked with arrows), rather like the two tendency notes in an ordinary dominant 7th chord.

Ex. 4.12.2

Four final points:

■ A tendency note should always be resolved in the **same** part.

■ The dissonant note in a 7th chord is the **7th above the root** – this will not be a 7th above the bass note if the chord has been inverted.

■ Because the 7th is in the bass in chord V⁷d, its resolution must also be in the bass. If you use V⁷d it is more or less inevitable that the next chord will be Ib, as seen in the last progression in Example 4.12.1.

■ In the very common progression V⁷–I, in which both chords are in root position, the resolution of the two tendency notes makes it impossible to include all notes of both chords when using four parts or fewer. You will need to omit the 5th (and instead double the root) in one or other of the two chords, as seen in the first two progressions shown in Example 4.12.1.

Activity 4.12

a Transpose Example 4.12.1 to the keys of G major, G minor, F major and C minor.

b How does chord V⁷ in G major compare with chord V⁷ in G minor?

5 Counterpoint

5.1 Introduction: what is counterpoint?

There is **counterpoint** when two or more parts have simultaneous melodies with clearly distinct rhythms. The listener is much more conscious of hearing different musical strands than in the kind of homophonic writing shown in Example 3.4.2 (on page 35) where the parts are identical in rhythm.

Here is an example of a **contrapuntal texture** ('contrapuntal' is the adjective which describes counterpoint):

Ex. 5.1   Bach: Two-part Invention, No. 13

Counterpoint may be a kind of opposite of homophony. But it is not useful to think of it as the opposite of harmony.

Let us expand on this a little. Our study of harmony began with the *vertical* (or simultaneous) aspects of music – the sounding together of different pitches to form harmonic intervals and chords. On the other hand our definition of counterpoint stresses the *horizontal* aspects of music. However, *harmony* – even in the most homophonic (or 'chordal') writing – concerns not only the vertical make-up of each chord, but also *progressions* of chords in which we must pay close attention to 'horizontal' part-writing (normally with plenty of stepwise movement and small leaps in upper parts, contrary motion for much of the time between melody and bass, and avoidance of consecutive 5ths and octaves).

Remember also that the various melodic ('horizontal') parts in contrapuntal writing do not just go their own ways without any regard for the resulting ('vertical') harmony. Look at Example 5.1 again and see how Bach bases his music on chords I and V^7 of A minor. Traditional counterpoint of this sort is based on the types of chords described in Chapter 2.

5.2 Some principles of counterpoint

In successful contrapuntal writing:

- The principles of part-writing referred to in Chapter 4 are perhaps even more important (if that's possible) than in homophonic textures.
- The various parts are genuinely independent of each other in rhythm for most of the time. There may be moments when two or more parts move together (for example in parallel 3rds or 6ths), but these should be fairly few in your own exercises.
- Parts often take it in turns to have the shorter note values. For instance, in Example 5.1, the right-hand part has shorter note values than the left to begin with, but this is reversed later.
- Each part has genuine melodic interest.

5.3 Making melodies interesting

What gives a melody musical interest? Here are five things that help.

- **Rhythmic variety and balance**

Few melodies are based for long on only one or two note values. However, placing very short and very long notes next to one another is rarely convincing. Sometimes shorter notes are used more frequently as a melody unfolds and as excitement grows (for example in the melody of Example 4.10.1 on page 61).

■ Balance between ascending and descending movement

A large leap is often followed by movement in the opposite direction. In Example 5.3.1 each rising interval is followed by a mainly stepwise fall. The resulting succession of descending phrases combines with the minor key and slow speed to create the nostalgic character of this famous melody.

Ex. 5.3.1
Adagio
Albinoni (arr. Giazotto): Adagio

■ Balance between stepwise movement and leaps

Melodies in most musical styles have a good deal of stepwise movement, but too much can be dull, and at least a few leaps are essential to give shape to a tune. For instance, see the melody of *Moon River* quoted in Exercise 4.10.2 on page 62, where the leaps occur at the *start* of each descending phrase, rather than *after* each phrase, as they do in Example 5.3.1 above.

Too many wide leaps can create a disjointed effect of course. On the face of it, bar 2 of Corelli's cello part in Example 4.9.4 (page 60) seems over-active. But bass parts, which outline the harmonies, do generally have more leaps than other parts, and here the various octaves create additional movement against the smooth and stepwise violin parts.

■ Use of a reasonable range

In conventional melody writing, too much emphasis on a small number of pitches can sound tedious – it is as though the tune doesn't seem to be getting anywhere. In many instrumental melodies the composer deliberately exploits the player's ability to cover a considerable range of notes, and may therefore use much wider intervals than singers could manage.

This means knowing the range of the instruments for which you write, and also understanding a little about the different parts of that range. For example, although the flute can go as low as middle C, the bottom notes are quiet and easily masked by other instruments. In contrast, it can produce a clear, bright tone in its upper register, starting from D, a 9th above middle C, and continuing well into the leger lines above the treble stave. Flute parts generally sound better if kept fairly high.

Details about the ranges of various instruments are given on pages 124–125.

■ Satisfying structure

Composers give much thought to structuring their melodies. Repetition of a good idea makes a tune memorable, but exact repetition risks sounding boring and is often avoided. At bar 5 of *Moon River* (page 62), Mancini doesn't do the obvious and repeat all of the first four bars. Instead he starts with a repetition of bars 3–4 only, and then adds a new ending to complete his second four-bar phrase.

The melody in Example 5.3.1 above uses **varied repetition** in a different way. The second phrase (bars 3–4) is the same as the first, except that it is one step higher. This is known as a melodic **sequence** and it has the side effect of making the first phrase end on the leading-note (F♯) and the second phrase 'answer' it by ending on the tonic (G), thus satisfying the tendency of the leading note to rise to the tonic, although only after a tantalising gap in this example.

Too many sequences can sound as predictable as straight repetition, so the third phrase is considerably varied, but the basic scalic descent of the opening idea is still present in the notes G–F–E♭–D, despite the decoration with other pitches. The overall shape of a melody is also important. We have already noticed that Example 5.3.1 consists of a succession of descending phrases. More optimistic melodies will often use ascending phrases. 'Arch' shapes are also widely used. In these the highest note may come near the start (as in *Moon River*), in the middle or near (but not at) the end.

Phrase construction

Play or sing the following well-known melody. It has four phrases of equal length, each with the same rhythm (slightly varied at the end of the third phrase).

Ex. 5.3.2   Mildred J. Hill: *Happy Birthday to You!*

- The first phrase establishes the rhythmic pattern of the song and rises to end on the leading note of F major.

- The second phrase is almost the same as the first, but at the end it rises one step higher, giving the sense that the tune is moving forward. By ending on the tonic it provides an answer to the first phrase and resolves its leading note.

- The third phrase uses the rhythm of the first two phrases (slightly varied at the end). It uses the same first two pitches, but after these it immediately leaps to a climactic top note, balanced by a descent in the rest of the phrase.

- The fourth phrase also uses the rhythm of the first two phrases. Again it begins with a pair of quavers of identical pitch, but this concluding phrase starts high and then descends to end on the tonic.

Activity 5.3

Using the above commentary as a model, describe how each of the following tunes is constructed. Identify climactic points and mention examples of varied repetition.

Arlen: *Somewhere Over the Rainbow*

Bach / Petzold (attrib.): *Minuet in G*

Brahms: *Cradle Song*

5.4 Imitation

If you have ever sung rounds such as *Three Blind Mice* or *London's Burning*, you will have heard **imitation**. It occurs when a melodic idea in one part is immediately taken up by another, while the first part continues. In the following round, first published in 1609, the second and third voices imitate the first part.

Ex. 5.4.1 — Ravenscroft: *Pammelia*

Imitation is often used in contrapuntal textures, although sometimes only for a few notes at a time. Look back to Example 5.1 on page 64 and notice how the left hand twice imitates the semiquaver patterns previously heard in the right hand.

In Example 5.4.1 above, the second voice enters at the same pitch as the first, and the bass is also the same, except for being an octave lower.

This is not always the case. In Example 5.4.2 below, the **imitative entry** in the second part is a 4th lower than the same tune in the upper part, while in Example 5.4.3 the lower part enters first, and then the upper part imitates it a 5th higher. We could think of these as tonic- and dominant-based entries, and they are at least as common as imitation at the unison or octave.

Ex. 5.4.2 — Bach: Fugue in C, BWV 846

Ex. 5.4.3 — Bach: Fugue in C, BWV 846

Notice that in Example 5.4.2, the imitative part enters after only two beats (known as close imitation) while in Example 5.4.3 the imitation occurs six beats later. But in both cases the imitation is *exact* – in other words, all the intervals of the melody are the same in the imitated version, despite the difference in pitch.

Imitation is not always exact. In Example 5.4.4 on the next page, there are several differences between the vocal melody and its imitation in the accompaniment.

Interval **A**, originally a minor 2nd, becomes a minor 3rd when imitated and the triadic shape **B** becomes a stepwise descent. But we still hear this as imitation because the pitch outline is similar enough and, most importantly, the rhythm remains the same.

Ex. 5.4.4

Bernstein: 'Somewhere' from *West Side Story*

There's a   time for us,   Some day a   time   for us,

The reason for inexact imitation may be, as in this example, that the composer wants certain harmonies more than he wants exact imitation. Whether exact or inexact, imitation must make sense with the harmonies in the other parts.

Another reason is to allow a tonic–dominant shape in one part to be answered by a dominant–tonic shape in another, without causing unwanted modulation. The melody at the start of Example 5.4.5 begins with a lower auxiliary spanning a tone between the notes G and F, and then leaps down a 5th from dominant to tonic. When this is imitated a 4th higher, the lower auxiliary spans only a semitone (between C and B) and the melody then leaps down a 4th from tonic to the dominant below:

Ex. 5.4.5

Bach: Fugue in C, BWV 870

This is known as a **tonal answer**, because the changes keep the music within the same key. If Bach had used a **real answer**, in which the imitation exactly copies the intervals of the subject, the music would have started heading towards F major, as shown right, which would have been an unlikely key for a first modulation.

Imitation is often described in terms of the intervals separating the original and imitating parts. For example, the imitation in Example 5.4.2 is at the 4th below, in Example 5.4.3 it is at the 5th above, and in Example 5.4.4 it is at the octave above.

Activity 5.4

Draw brackets under the lower part in this passage of 16th-century music to show how the upper part has been imitated. Identify the interval of imitation in all three cases, and state which imitation is exact and which is the least exact of the three.

Taverner: *Gaude plurimum* (text omitted)

5.5 Canon

In a **canon** exact imitation continues for a considerable time (perhaps throughout a whole section or piece). Canon is often considered a rather learned device, and it does require considerable skill, but most people know a few simple canons, such as *Three Blind Mice*, *London's Burning* or *Frère Jacques*. These are all a type of canon known as a round, because you can keep the canon going round indefinitely by returning to the beginning of the melody as soon as you reach the end.

Other types of canon don't keep repeating like rounds, and they may be combined with other non-imitative parts within the contrapuntal texture.

The right-hand part of Example 5.5 shows the beginning of a two-part canon. The left-hand part is clearly contrapuntal, but it does not take part in the canon. Instead it provides a **free part** that supports the canon and makes the harmonic structure clearer and the texture fuller.

Ex. 5.5

Bach: *Goldberg* Variations, No. 6

Notice how the use of sequence as well as canon binds this passage together, and how Bach is able to cover a wide range by making his bass part surge upward in contrary motion to the canonic parts, which plummet down across two octaves.

Bach was the most skilful of composers at working contrapuntal textures into brilliant and attractive pieces, and he was at the height of his powers when this music was first published in 1741. No composer has achieved quite such a reputation for contrapuntal skill in the more than two-and-a-half centuries since then.

Imitative and canonic textures are found less often in the Classical style of the late 18th century and in the Romantic style of the 19th century, but canonic writing really came back into favour in 20th-century serialism.

Finally, note that canon is described in the same way as imitation – by naming the interval between the parts ('at the 5th below', and so on). So we can say that Example 5.5 includes a canon at the 2nd above.

6 Analysis of harmony

This chapter will be helpful for anyone requiring information on simple harmonic analysis.

6.1 Analysis: what is it and why do it?

Analysis of any kind involves:

- Examining something in detail to understand its workings
- Using these findings to discover general principles.

You may think that analysing music could reduce your enjoyment of it, or at best be a pointless activity. After all, music is intended to be listened to, not dissected. However, understanding how something works will generally enrich our experience of it. For instance, would watching a football match or any other team game really hold your attention if you knew nothing about the rules or what the opposing players are trying to do?

But it is important not to get bogged down in the detail. When analysing we should always try to see the bigger picture – to understand how the relationship between chords defines a key or allows the music to move between keys, how the use of non-chord notes can give life to a melody and make the music more expressive, and how the structure of a piece relates to the keys through which it passes.

6.2 Adding Roman numerals (1)

You have added Roman numerals to chords before, as in **Activity 3.19**, but we shall now look at such labelling in greater detail. This is necessary because Roman numerals feature in some examination tasks and in many published writings about music. Roman numerals are not the be-all and end-all of music analysis of course, but they are very valuable in showing how chords work within a key – in describing the **functions** of chords. It's not wrong to refer to chords by letter names such as Em or G^{maj7}, as many musicians do all the time, but in isolation such symbols don't tell us much about the harmonic function of the chords that they represent.

Before you can add Roman numerals to the chords in a piece of music, you need to work out the key, as explained on the next page. Then you will probably find it useful – especially in the early stages – to make a chart of the triads in that key. It's a good idea to include the 7ths for at least chords II^7 and V^7. Write out the letter names of each chord *from the bass up*, as in this example for the chords of G major:

	Inversion letter						
7th	(d)		(G)		(C)		
5th	(c)	D	E	F♯	G	A	B	C
3rd	(b)	B	C	D	E	F♯	G	A
root		G	A	B	C	D	E	F♯
	G major:	I	ii$^{(7)}$	iii	IV	V$^{(7)}$	vi	vii

Ex. 6.2.1   Melody: Anglo-Genevan Psalms, 1558

Identifying the key

Here's a method for identifying the main key of a piece, which we have applied to Example 6.2.1 above:

- Look at the key signature:

  The example has a key signature of one sharp.

- Name the two keys that share this key signature – a major key and its relative minor (if necessary, revise key signatures: see pages 9, 13 and 122):

  A key signature of one sharp belongs to G major and E minor.

- To decide between the two possibilities, look for the raised seventh degree of a minor key (in E minor this would be D♯):

  There is no D♯ in Example 6.2.1 – every D is D♮.

- In the absence of any other evidence, the key will be the major key suggested by the key signature:

  Example 6.2.1 appears to be in G major.

- Check your findings by looking for a perfect (or imperfect) cadence in the key you have chosen:

  In Example 6.2.1 there is a perfect cadence in G major in bars 3^4–4^1. This key is also confirmed by the fact that both melody and bass end on G in bar 4.

This method works well with short excerpts and simple pieces, but things are less easy if the music changes key or includes chromatic notes. However, we'll leave such complications until later.

Labelling triads

Now let's see how to label the chord at bar 2^1 in the example above:

- List the notes in the chord *from the bass up*, ignoring any doubled notes: $\begin{smallmatrix}F\sharp\\A\\D\end{smallmatrix}$

- Find this set of notes in your chord chart – $\begin{smallmatrix}F\sharp\\A\\D\end{smallmatrix}$ is the same as $\begin{smallmatrix}A\\F\sharp\\D\end{smallmatrix}$ – in other words it is chord V of G major

- Is the bass note of the chord the same as the root of chord V on your chart? In this case it is, and so the chord in bar 2^1 is V in root position.

Let's label another chord – this time the one at bar 1^4:

- List the notes in the chord *from the bass up*, ignoring any doubled notes: $\begin{smallmatrix}C\\G\\E\end{smallmatrix}$

- Find this set of notes in your chord chart – $\begin{smallmatrix}C\\G\\E\end{smallmatrix}$ is the same as $\begin{smallmatrix}G\\E\\C\end{smallmatrix}$, in other words it is chord IV of G major

- Is the bass note of the chord the same as the root of chord IV on your chart? In this case it is not. The bass note of the chord is E, which is the 3rd of chord IV. The chord is therefore in first inversion and so we label it as IVb.

If you are unsure about using letters to show inverted chords, revise the information on page 25.

Activity 6.2.1

a We have identified the two chords in bars 1⁴–2¹ of Example 6.2.1. What type of cadence do they form?

b Label the remaining chords in Example 6.2.1, using the method described on the previous page.

In the next example the **harmonic rhythm** is more varied – that is, the rate of chord change is less regular – and the music introduces several important new points about labelling chords. The key is F major – make a chord chart for F major now, in preparation for the next activity.

Ex. 6.2.2   English traditional melody

F major: I   vi

Repeated notes

The chord on the first quaver of bar 1 is repeated on the second quaver. Less obviously, this is the same chord (F major) as the crotchet upbeat at the start of the passage – it is just the layout of the upper parts that is different. There is generally no need to label chords that have been repeated like this.

Something similar occurs in beats 2 and 3 of bar 1. Even though the tenor moves between D and A, and the other parts repeat their notes on the last quaver of the bar, the only notes sounded are D, F and A – so a chord of D minor sounds throughout the second and third beats of bar 1.

Sustained notes

The white boxes indicate notes that are sustained while other parts move. These notes must be taken into account if the chord around them changes, as it does on the second quavers of bars 2 and 3.

Missing 5ths

On the beat marked * there are only two pitches (F and A). These could be part of chord I (F–A–C) or chord vi (D–F–A). Which is it? On page 31 we learned that the 5th of a chord can be omitted, so chord I (without a C) would be the correct choice – especially since it is preceded by chord V, creating a perfect cadence. If it were chord vi, the root (D) would be missing, which would be highly unusual.

Passing notes

The note marked ** on the last quaver of bar 3 is a passing note – a note that moves by step between two harmony notes a 3rd apart. As explained on page 55, this is a type of **non-chord note**, and can therefore be ignored when labelling chords.

Activity 6.2.2

Label all of the chords in Example 6.2.2 – remember that the key is F major.

The music for **Activity 6.2.3** below is printed on three staves, since it comes from a song for voice and piano. Much music is written or printed on more than two staves. The method of identifying chords is still the same as in (for instance) Example 6.2.2, but you must take into account the notes on *all* staves.

Activity 6.2.3

a Name the key of the following passage and identify the chords by writing in the boxes below the bass stave. All of the chords are triads, either in root position, first inversion or second inversion.

b Draw a circle round the only example of a passing note in the passage.

Gerald Lane: *Tatters* (adapted)

Key: _____

6.3 Adding Roman numerals (2)

The following passage includes four dominant 7th chords in C major:

Ex. 6.3   Melody by M Vulpius (1609)

(1)   (2)   (3)   (4)

Labelling a dominant 7th is done in the same way as for a triad, but remember that in addition to a root position (V^7) it has *three* inversions (V^7b, V^7c and V^7d).

Make a chord chart for C major, similar to the one on page 70, and then write down the letter names, *from the bass up*, of the chord in bar 3^3 (shown in a white box). Don't forget to include the tenor D that is held on from the previous beat. Notice that there are no doubled notes in this chord, which is not surprising since 7th chords have *four* different notes, not three like triads.

Now find out where the bass note of the shaded chord occurs within the notes of V^7 on your chord chart. It is F, and you can see from the part of the chart shown right that this has the inversion letter 'd'. You can now label the chord correctly as V^7d.

7th	(d)	(F)
5th	(c)	D
3rd	(b)	B
root		G
C major:		$V^{(7)}$

Activity 6.3

a Identify the dominant-7th chords in Example 6.3 by completing the blanks in the following list. In chord (2) the soprano and tenor notes are sustained from the previous beat and must be taken into account when labelling the chord.

(1) _____ (2) _____ (3) ____ V^7d ____ (4) _____

b Identify the key of the following passage, make yourself a chord chart for that key, and then label the chords. As well as chord V^7 this piece includes chord ii^7, another very common type of 7th chord. There is a tierce de Picardie at the end – label the final chord $I^{\sharp3}$ to show this.

H Benham: Psalm chant

c One other 7th chord that you may need to identify is the diminished 7th (discussed on page 29). The following extract includes an example (chord vii^7) as well as another instance of chord ii^7b.

Name the key of the following passage and then label each of its chords. Also write 'dim^7' below the chord you identify as vii^7. Remember that you don't need to take account of the shaded passing notes when identifying the chords.

Bach: Chorale 356 (adapted)

Key: _____

6.4 Melodic decoration

We have already seen that passing notes don't affect the labelling of chords. The same applies to auxiliaries and anticipations, both of which we encountered in Chapter 4, and to another type of non-chord note that we haven't previously encountered. This is the **échappée**, or 'escape note'. It leaves a harmony note by step (usually upwards) and then leaps in the opposite direction (usually by a 3rd) to a new harmony note:

Ex. 6.4.1   Bach: Chorale 103

échappée

Other types of melodic decoration – accented passing notes, appoggiaturas and suspensions – generally coincide with the start of a chord. Because we hear a note that's not part of the new chord, we can't match the notes heard with those in a typical chord diagram.

For instance, the notes at the start of bar 2 in Example 6.4.2 below are C, F and G – which don't exactly match any triad or 7th chord in F major. But the chord which follows it contains C, E and G (the last of these sustained by the soprano from the first beat of the bar). This is chord V of F major. This implies that the alto F in bar 2^1 is not a chord note. To be precise, it is a suspension, with its resolution at bar 2^2 (and a preparation at bar 1^4.) The alto's F– E in the first half of bar 2 forms the intervals of a 4th followed by a 3rd above the bass C, and we can therefore label the chord in this part of the bar as V^{4-3}:

Ex. 6.4.2   Traditional: *Stabat Mater*

F major: iib   vi   V   Ib V^{4-3} I

Ex. 6.4.3   Mozart, Sonata in E♭, K. 282

pp

E♭ major: Ic V^7 I

If you are unsure about suspensions, revise pages 58–60. Appoggiaturas were discussed on pages 61-62 and accented passing notes on page 56.

A rather more complicated suspension is shown in Example 6.4.3 above. All three upper parts in chord V^7 hang on to their notes (shown by the white box) while the bass moves to I. This creates a triple suspension over chord I, a favourite harmonic device of composers in the Classical period. It creates a powerful dissonance on the strong third beat of the bar, which is released when the three upper parts resolve to their own notes in chord I on the weak fourth beat. The chord on beat 3 could be labelled as $V^7/_I$ to show this effect.

Activity 6.4

a The following passage is in B♭ major and all of the chords are already labelled. Identify the function of each of the five notes marked * by writing one of the following abbreviations above each of these notes:

PN (passing note)   A (anticipation)   AUX (auxiliary note)
E (échappée)   S (suspension)   H (additional harmony note)

G F Root: *Tramp! Tramp! Tramp!* (adapted)

B♭ major: V   I   IV   I   IV   V   I

b Name the key of the following passage, and then identify the six numbered chords. Also state the function (e.g. anticipation) of each of the notes lettered A to H. Write your answers on the lines beneath the music.

Bach: Chorale 153

Key: _____

Chords:

1 _____

2 _____

3 _____

4 _____

5 _____

6 _____

Notes of melodic decoration

A _____

B _____

C _____

D _____

E _____

F _____

G _____

H _____

c Name the key of the following extract and label the four chords marked by a bracket. Also identify *two* suspensions later in the passage by writing appropriate pairs of figures (e.g. 7-6) above or below the notes concerned.

Melody adapted from Störl's *Württemberg Gesangbuch* (1710)

Chords

Key: _____

d Complete the labelling of the chords in this passage, name the type of melodic decoration (e.g. anticipation) produced by each of the four notes marked A–D, and explain how the tonic chord marked * has been decorated.

Mozart: Sonata K. 545 (ii)

G major: | I | | | | | | | I |

6.5 Piano textures and implied chords

Most of our examples so far have been in four-part harmony, but now it is time to look at music in which the textures can be more varied, although the principles of harmonic analysis that we have learned will still apply.

In piano music the number of parts is often not constant. So although some chords in Example 6.5.1 below have four parts, others have three, and there is a two-part passage where left-hand chords are split into arpeggio patterns. Occasionally the melody stands alone, but even here harmony is still implied. For example, when the left hand rests in bars 1–2, the C major chord it has already established continues to be outlined by the right-hand melody:

Ex. 6.5.1
Allegro con brio
Haydn: Sonata in C (Hob. XVI:35)

Most chords in the example above are easy to identify, although you need to be alert to the change of left-hand clef from bar 5 onwards (a feature found in many piano pieces). However, in a few cases we must consider what chord the composer *implied*. Look at the first half of bar 7, where the only notes are F in the bass and D in the melody. These occur in all three chords shown right: which one does Haydn imply?

The clue is to look at what happens next – the chord is followed by a perfect cadence. We know from our work on page 36 that these are often approached by a chord from the subdominant group, with iib being particularly common. This would be a much more logical choice than the other two possibilities, which both come from the dominant group of chords.

Another two-note chord appears in bar 12. Why have we labelled this as Vb rather than *vii*, especially since the root of Vb (which is G) doesn't even appear in the chord? Again, the clue is the cadential position of the chord. It ends a phrase and so the ear expects a cadence (which is provided by the progression I–Vb) rather than for the music just to stop in mid-air on chord *vii*.

Notice that while a tonic chord lasts throughout bars 1–2 and bars 8–10, the rate of harmonic change increases to two chords per bar as cadences approach. This is a good principle to follow in your own work when writing in tonal styles. The C heard in the bass on every beat in bars 8–10 is *not* a pedal because the chords don't change above it. However, the G heard at the top of each of the left-hand broken chords in bars 8–11 does function as a simple **inner pedal**, because we briefly hear chord V⁷c above it, as well as plenty of chord I.

> **For more on the various types of pedal, see page 43.**

While sparse-textured piano writing often includes chords that are merely implied, fuller textures have complications of their own because many notes are likely to be doubled. Chopin begins the piano prelude in Example 6.5.2 below in a very grand and resonant manner, his use of mid- and low-range notes adding to the weight and solemnity. There are at least six notes at once, but actually no more than four real parts, as can be seen in Example 6.5.3, in which the doublings have been stripped out, leaving a texture that could be sung by SATB voices:

Ex. 6.5.2 — Chopin: Prelude Op. 28 No. 20. Largo. *ff* *solenne*. con Ped.

Ex. 6.5.3 — *passing note*, *appoggiatura*. C minor: I   IV   V   I

Incidentally, in Example 6.5.2 Chopin is not guilty of consecutive octaves in the left hand or between top and bottom notes of the right hand. These octaves are purposeful, consistent doublings for additional sonority, not isolated mistakes. Such octave doubling is found in much piano and orchestral writing.

Activity 6.5

Name the key and identify each bracketed chord in the two following passages. Also mark all non-chord notes with X. Notice the left-hand clef in the first extract.

Allegro — Mozart: Sonata in C, K. 545

Allegro non troppo
la melodia con molto espressione — Tchaikovsky: *Chanson triste*, Op. 40 No. 2
p

6.6 Other textures

Much music is notated on three staves – songs, pieces for solo instrument and keyboard, Baroque trio sonatas, and so on. Studying a score with three staves takes a little more time, but harmonic analysis is the same in every essential respect however many staves there are.

The following extract comes from a song. There are two staves for piano, and one for voice. Always check the clefs carefully before starting your analysis.

Ex. 6.6.1 — Schubert: *Wasserflut*

This example is even more densely textured than the Chopin extract on the previous page, for there are seven or eight notes sounding at once. But so many notes are only the result of much doubling. For instance, A and C each appear three times in the first chord, and E appears twice. Notice that the music, although so rich in texture, is extremely quiet. Additional fullness doesn't necessarily mean additional volume.

Four staves at once are used in scores of string quartets and in music for SATB voices written in open score (with one part per stave instead of the two per stave used in short score). Vocal music in open score normally uses the treble clef for the soprano, alto and tenor parts and the bass clef for the lowest part. The tenors actually sing their part an octave lower – a small 8 is often attached below the clef as a reminder of this.

Scores of string quartets adopt a similar format, except that the 'tenor' part is played on a viola – an instrument that uses a C clef (with middle C on the middle line), except where the notes are high enough for the treble clef to be more convenient. Similarly, the cello may leave the bass clef for high passages, which are written in the tenor C clef (in which the second line from the top is middle C), or even the treble clef for notes in the highest register.

The following examples show the same bar of music laid out in three ways – short score, open score, and scored for string quartet:

Ex. 6.6.2 — Handel: *Messiah*; Ex. 6.6.3 — Handel: *Messiah*; Ex. 6.6.4 — Handel: *Messiah*

Scores for orchestra or band may involve far more than four staves at a time, but often the harmony is still in only four parts. If you're aiming to identify a chord in a full score of this type, important steps include locating the bass part and deciding which parts are just doublings.

When looking for the bass part, remember that double basses sound an octave lower than written – so the lowest note on paper may not necessarily be the lowest note that is heard. There are also likely to be a number of other transposing instruments, such as clarinets, saxophones, horns and trumpets, whose sounding pitch is different from their written pitch. Identifying chords in full scores is beyond the scope of this book, but a useful tip for making analysis easier is to transcribe any chord that is puzzling you onto a two-stave score, as if for piano, with every note at sounding pitch.

Activity 6.6

a Identify the bracketed chords in the following excerpt from a Baroque trio sonata. Also, for each of the three suspensions, write S where the suspension sounds, and add the appropriate figuring (e.g. 9–8) to your Roman numerals.

Corelli: Sonata Op. 1 No. 8 (opening)

b To answer this question you will need to be able to read the alto clef used for the viola part, in which the middle line of the stave represents middle C. Name the key and identify the nine chords in this passage. Then label each non-chord note in the first violin part as AUX (auxiliary note), PN (passing note), S (suspension) or APP (appoggiatura).

Mozart: String Quartet in E♭, K. 428

c Name the key and identify the chords in the following song.

Devonshire folk song

6.7 Accidentals and modulation

We learned on page 48 that accidentals can have different functions.

They may be:

- The raised or lowered versions of notes 6 and 7 in a minor key
- Chromatic alterations used to decorate the music without changing key
- The pitches needed for a new key because the music has modulated.

When analysing harmony, it is essential to work out if accidentals are part of a modulation to a new key, because this will alter the way chords are identified. For instance, a chord of G major is chord V if the key is C major, but chord I if the key is G major. To work out if a note with an accidental is chromatic or not, look for a cadence at, or shortly after, the note concerned:

- In Example 6.7.1 below there is an F♯, but the cadence is V–I in C major, with a passing note on F♮. There is therefore no modulation and so F♯ is chromatic.

- In Example 6.7.2 the cadence is V⁷– I in G major. The cadence confirms that the music has modulated to G major and so F♯ is *not* chromatic.

- In Example 6.7.3 the cadence is V⁷–I in G *minor*. F♯ is the raised leading note of that key, so F♯ is not chromatic and neither is there a modulation.

A change of key doesn't always involve accidentals. For example, a modulation from C major to G major needs F♯, but a modulation back to C only requires that F is no longer sharpened – there may not always be a need for a natural sign before the F to indicate this. Look at the first example on page 47. It starts in B minor, hence the presence of A♯ (the raised leading note) and a cadence in B minor in bars 4³–5¹. But after that the note A is no longer sharpened – all of the notes come from the key of D major, and the cadence in that key in bars 7³–8 confirms that the piece has indeed modulated from B minor to its relative major, D major.

We will look at modulation in more detail in **Section 6.10**.

6.8 Chromatic decoration

Chromatic notes can be non-chord notes (such as passing notes and auxiliary notes) or they can be part of the harmony. Here is a passage with eight chromatic notes – the underlying chords are shown (notice that the left-hand starts in the treble clef). After hearing the passage as printed, try listening to it played with every accidental ignored – a brutal but effective way of finding out how much the music's character owes to a well-judged use of chromatic notes.

Ex. 6.8

Mozart: Sonata in C, K. 279

Here is an analysis of the eight chromatic notes marked in this extract:

1 C♯ is a chromatic appoggiatura, resolving to D, over chord Vb in C major

2 C♯ here is a chromatic lower auxiliary note between two Ds, both harmony notes

3 D♯ is a chromatic appoggiatura, resolving to E, over chord I

4 The turn symbol indicates the pattern A–G–F♯–G, in which F♯ is a chromatic note

5 The B♭ is a chromatic harmony note (part of V⁷ of IV) – although note that the next chord of F major is not in root position as one might expect, but in second inversion.

6 G♯ is another chromatic appoggiatura, resolving to A over chord IVc

7 F♯ is our fourth chromatic appoggiatura, resolving to G over chord I

8 G♯ is a chromatic harmony note – the root of a diminished 7th chord which resolves to chord vi on the next beat, rather like a secondary dominant (see page 47) – again there is no sense of modulation because the music carries on in C major (and with G♯ cancelled by G♮) in the very next bar.

Activity 6.8

a Name the key of this extract and complete the labelling of the chords by writing in the boxes below the stave. Then write PN above each diatonic passing note, CPN above the one chromatic passing note (see box below), and APN above each accented passing note in the final (incomplete) bar.

Mozart: Sonata in C, K. 545

Key: _____   [ ] [ ] [ ] [ ] [ ] [ ] [V]

Chromatic passing notes move by semitone step between notes that are a tone apart.

b Name the key of the following passage and label each of the chords in bars 2–4. Then circle any chromatic notes and state what type of non-chord note they are. Notice that chord V⁷ is implied by the first eight notes of the melody.

Beethoven: *Klavierstück für Elise*

(V⁷_____)

Key: _____   Chords: _____   _____   _____

c Study the following passage and then complete the blanks in the commentary below.

[Rather slowly]

English traditional: *The Oak and the Ash*

'I ___ wish once a-gain in the North I could be'.

This passage is in the key of _____ . The three chords in bar 1 are _____ ,

_____ and _____ . The chord that lasts throughout the final incomplete

bar of the extract is chord _____ . The B♮ in the bass of bar 1 is a _____ ,

but the accidentals in the other parts of this bar are all _____ . In bar 2 the B♭ in the

vocal melody is a chromatic _____ note.

6.9 Chromatic chords: diminished 7ths

Probably the most common type of chromatic chord is the diminished 7th. (In fact, you have already come across an example in Example 6.8, bar 6.). In root position this has an interval of a diminished 7th between its outer notes, with each note of the chord a minor 3rd higher than the previous one. A diminished 7th on the leading note of a minor key (chord *vii⁷*) is actually diatonic (all of its notes occur within the key) but in other cases diminished 7ths are chromatic chords.

> For more on the *diatonic* diminished 7th chord, see **Section 2.13, page 29.**

The following example includes a chromatic diminished 7th at bar 1². The music is from a piece whose text has earlier dealt with the prospect of death, and its final movement is harmonically very tense, with the diminished 7th contributing to this. The chord is all the more striking because, unusually, every part moves upwards to it together (with simultaneous passing notes in all three upper parts) – there's no contrary, or even oblique, motion at all. The unusually high alto and tenor parts add further to the tension.

Ex. 6.9   Bach, Chorale 216

E major: I   IV   dim⁷   V⁴ ⁻ ³   I
                                      ₇

In simple analysis it is not usually necessary to give Roman numerals for chromatic diminished-7th chords – labelling such chords as 'diminished 7th' or 'dim⁷' is usually sufficient.

Activity 6.9

a In Example 6.9 above, name the type of melodic decoration used in

   (i) the soprano part at bar 1³ and

   (ii) the alto part on the second semiquaver of bar 1⁴.

b Identify the key of the following passage and draw a bracket (└─────┘) below the diminished-7th chord. How does Schubert depict the meaning of the text in this extract?

[Poco allegro ed energico]

Schubert: *Der stürmische Morgen*

der Win – ter kalt und wild.
the win – ter cold and wild.

ff

6.10 Identifying changes of key

Begin by revising **Sections 3.16** and **3.17**, which explain the *process* of modulation. Here we will look at *identifying* changes of key.

To identify the first modulation in a piece, ask these questions:

1 What is the key at the beginning of the piece?

2 What is the first note outside this key?

3 Does this note soon reappear, and/or is it part of a $V^{(7)}$–I cadence?

4 If yes, what key is suggested by this new note (and cadence)?
   If no, look for the next note outside the original key and repeat steps 3 and 4.

5 How is the new key related to the opening key (e.g. dominant, relative minor)?

We'll now apply this method to the music printed below:

Ex. 6.10.1

John Blow (from *Musick's Hand-maid*, 1689)

Saraband

1 The opening key is C major – there are no sharps or flats and this key is confirmed by a perfect cadence in C major in bar 4.

2 The first note outside this key is F♯ in bar 6.

3 F♯ reappears in bar 8, where it is part of a V– I cadence in G major. This is an important cadence since it marks the end of the first section of this binary-form structure.

4 The key suggested is therefore G major.

5 This new key is the dominant of the original key. In Baroque and Classical pieces that begin in a major key, a modulation to the dominant is very common at the end of the first main section.

The process for identifying subsequent modulations is similar, but you need to be alert to what happens to notes that have already been altered. For instance, in bar 10 above, F is no longer sharpened so this *could* herald a return to C major – but it doesn't since there is no cadence in this key. Look ahead and notice G♯ in bars 11 and 12. This suggests a modulation to A minor, and that is confirmed by the V– I cadence in A minor in bar 12. This new key is the relative minor of the original key of C major.

Finally look at bars 13–16. G is no longer sharpened, so this again might suggest a return to the tonic key, and this time it is confirmed by the V–I cadence in C major in the final bar. Always expect a modulation back to the tonic before the end, unless the music is just an extract from a longer piece.

If you need to label chords in a passage that has modulated, remember to state the new key and make sure that you base your Roman numerals on the new key for the passage concerned. For instance, Example 6.10.2 below starts in G major, so chord I will be G, but its second phrase is in D major, where chord I will be D.

Notice that when a pivot chord (see page 46) is used, it is usually given two Roman numerals – one in the old key and the other in the new key – as in bar 4⁴ below.

Ex. 6.10.2   Handel: Flute Sonata, Op. 1 No. 5
Bourrée

G major: I   Vb   I iiib vi   IV   Ib IV   Vb I iib V⁷   I   V
                                                              D major: I

(D:)   IV   viib   V   I   Ib   V   I

To make a modulation really stick, it's useful to cadence in the new key more than once. There are three V–I progressions in D major in bars 5–8 above. The first and second are deliberately inconclusive but the third is much stronger and more final-sounding.

Activity 6.10

a In Example 6.10.2 above, identify the four chords in bar 6, noting carefully the key of the music at this point.

b Give the correct term (e.g. échappée or appoggiatura) for each of the following types of melodic decoration in Example 6.10.2 above.

The notes marked **A** _____

The notes marked **B** _____

The note marked **C** _____

c Study the following passage of music and then complete the commentary below.

Haydn: *Tedesca*, Hob. IX/22 No. 3

This extract begins and ends in the key of _____ . In bars 3–4 there is a perfect

cadence (Vb–I) in the key of _____ . The notes C♯ and A♯ in bars 2 and 6 are

chromatic _____ notes.

d Name the key and cadence in each of the bracketed phrases below. Also, circle a lower
auxiliary note in the vocal part and explain how the chord marked * on the first beat of
bar 12 has been decorated.

With spirit

English air, *Down Among the Dead Men*

7 Harmonising a melody – short examples

This chapter shows you how to harmonise short melodies, beginning with cadences. This is useful for everyone studying harmony, but especially for those preparing to harmonise chorale melodies in the style of J S Bach (an option for the 2016 Pearson A level Music specification, for example).

However, please do remember that this chapter itself is not 'style-specific' – it does not deal directly with the Bach style of chorale harmonisation or with any other particular genre or style. It seeks to show you the broad harmonic and part-writing principles and procedures underlying much simple Baroque, Classical and Romantic music.

We shall be concentrating on four-part vocal harmony (for soprano, alto, tenor and bass). This is a useful preparation for chorale harmonisation – and its principles underlie many other types of writing.

7.1 Principles of harmonisation

To harmonise a melody we must first:

■ Identify the key and any changes of key

■ Know the chords for the key(s) involved (using chord charts, if that helps).

Then we:

■ Choose suitable chords, beginning with cadences and starts of phrases

■ Add the bass part and check that it works well with the melody

■ Add chord symbols underneath the bass part (if that's required and/or we find it useful)

■ Add parts for alto and tenor, if required, choosing appropriate notes to fit the soprano and bass, and shaping the inner parts to avoid errors such as consecutive 5ths, and to make them as attractive and singable as possible.

When you're used to this method, you'll probably find that choosing chords, adding the bass part and adding chord symbols can be done more or less simultaneously, rather than as three separate operations.

Suitable chords must fit the notes of the given melody. This means that each chord will need to include the melody note above it, although there may well be the opportunity to treat some melody notes as either unaccented dissonances, such as passing notes, or on-beat dissonances, such as appoggiaturas and suspensions.

Which of the available chords we choose, and whether we use a root position or an inversion, depends on the context. Chapter 3 (Chord Progressions) helps here, but we must also learn by remembering what composers have done in the past, and by playing (and playing about with) chords for ourselves.

At every stage, play or sing the exercises that you write, but also try to hear them in your head. Constantly check for accuracy and musical interest. Regard every bit of harmonisation, however humble, as an exercise in the art of composing. After all, composing is what we do when we harmonise: it is the putting together of notes in a purposeful and musical way.

7.2 What is the key of the melody?

An unharmonised melody may have fewer clues about its key than the harmonised textures we worked with in Chapter 6. Nevertheless, there's rarely much difficulty:

■ Many melodies begin on a note of the tonic chord, or with a dominant–tonic anacrusis like the one in **Activity 6.4** on page 75

■ Most melodies end on the tonic, although some finish on one of the other notes of the tonic chord (the 3rd or 5th).

Some exercises in harmonisation include the lower parts at the start, to help you identify the key and to give an idea of the required style.

There can be ambiguous moments – for example, the tune below can most conveniently be heard in E♭ major, but we could think in terms of C minor if we looked only at the start. There's no B♭ until bar 4, and also a C minor triad is outlined in bar 2.

Ex. 7.2.1

English air

I'm __ lone - some since I crossed the hill, And o'er the moor _ and _ val - ley

Remember that you should always try to verify a key by looking for cadences in that key. In an unharmonised melody, the cadence points may be suggested by the ends of phrase marks, pause signs or, if there are words, by line endings in the text. If there are few obvious clues to the position of cadences, remember that many simple pieces have a structure of balanced phrases, each lasting for two, four or eight bars. For example, the following melody is four bars long, its first phrase lasting for two complete bars. The two notes before the tick below are therefore the most likely place for the first cadence in the melody:

Ex. 7.2.2

Bach: Chorale 26

Note that Example 7.2.2, like many other melodies, does not begin at the start of a bar or finish at the end of a bar, but that each phrase still lasts for two complete bars (or eight crotchet beats).

You will need to work out the function of any accidentals in a melody that you are going to harmonise. Remember that accidentals could be:

- The raised or lowered forms of the sixth and seventh degrees of the scale
- An indication that the music has modulated
- Chromatic decoration that doesn't affect the key.

As always, look for possible cadences in order to verify any apparent change of key. The following melody begins in F major but ends in C major. The latter is indicated by two B♮s and verified by an ending that would support a V–I cadence in C major:

Ex. 7.2.3

Bach: Chorale 284

However, unharmonised melodies sometimes *imply* changes of key instead of stating them explicitly by using accidentals. When Bach harmonised the melody below, he treated the second phrase in C major, the dominant. The scalic descent to C was enough to suggest C major to him, despite the lack of a B♮ in the melody. Of course, B♮ appears in the harmony he added, to create the V–I cadence in C major.

Ex. 7.2.4

Bach: Chorale 323

C major: V   I

Incidentally, Bach could also have ended the first phrase in C major by harmonising its cadence (D–C in bar 2²⁻³) with a V–I progression in C. However, he stayed in F major at this early point in the piece, using a plagal cadence; in so doing he was later able to achieve valuable variety both in terms of keys and cadences.

Activity 7.2

a Name the key of the following melody. The key signature of two flats points either to B♭ major or G minor. The accidentals (together with the starting and finishing notes, and the likely perfect cadence in bars 8–9) make it easy to decide which.

L Marchand: *Fugue*

b Name the key of the melody below. There are no accidentals, but look at the first and last notes and consider which key would allow a perfect cadence to be written beneath the last two notes.

C H H Parry: *Intercessor*

c Name the main key of the following melody. Identify the two other keys visited in the third stave. How is each of these keys related to the overall key of the song?

Irish air: *The Minstrel Boy*

The   Min - strel Boy _ to the war has gone, In the ranks of   death you'll find   him, His

fa - ther's sword he has gir - ded   on, And his wild harp slung _ be - hind   him;

'Land of   song!' said the war - rior bard, 'Tho' all   the world be - trays ___ thee, One

sword   at least _ thy _ rights shall guard, One _ faith - ful harp _ shall _ praise thee!'

7.3 Harmonising cadences

It's sensible to begin a harmonisation by planning the cadences. They are vital in defining the key, and are mostly quite easy to deal with. In traditional tonal music there are four main types of cadence, two of which (perfect and imperfect) are by far the most common.

When you harmonise a cadence:

- Decide what type it is and label the chords

- Work out the bass notes. Contrary motion with the melody is often possible and desirable – but note that in Example 7.3.1 (iv) below similar motion enables the bass to move to the *lower* tonic, which can be useful in providing additional weight at an important perfect cadence.

    - If the cadence is perfect (V$^{(7)}$–I), interrupted (usually V$^{(7)}$–VI) or plagal (IV–I) this should be easy.

    - If the cadence is imperfect, the second chord will be V but the first chord needs to be chosen with care – the recommendations later in this section cover most cases

- Add the alto and tenor parts.

The following guidelines will help you match common melodic patterns to different types of cadence. They are shown in just a few of the many different spacings and keys that are possible. No matter how many tips people give you, however, you've still got to judge for yourself what works and what doesn't, and be prepared for the occasional cadence that doesn't quite fit any formula. Harmonisation isn't the musical equivalent of painting by numbers.

Perfect and interrupted cadences

Phrases that end with the melody falling by step to the tonic (2–1) or rising by step to the upper tonic (7–8) are most commonly harmonised with a perfect cadence, the first chord of which may be V^7 or just plain chord V:

Ex. 7.3.1

Because perfect cadences tend to appear frequently in most types of music, you can introduce variety in any of the following ways (illustrated in the next example):

- Using a first inversion for one of the two chords (but not both)
- Using the progression V^{7}d–Ib to create another type of inverted cadence
- Substituting chord vi for chord I to create an interrupted cadence.

These alternatives *are best reserved for intermediate cadences* – perfect cadences at the ends of main sections are usually V$^{(7)}$–I with both chords in root position.

Ex. 7.3.2

Bb major: V   Ib | D major: Vb   I | C minor: V⁷d   ib | A major: V⁷   vi

Other common melodic patterns at cadences are 2–3 and 5–3 (often separated by a passing note to give 5–4–3), both of which will fit perfect cadences. If you encounter 5–5 (a repeated dominant) it can be harmonised by either a perfect cadence (shown in cadence (iv) below) or an imperfect cadence. Your choice should depend on what sounds best in the context.

Ex. 7.3.3

G major: V   I | F major: V   I | A minor: V   i | E minor: V   i

Imperfect cadences

A phrase that ends on a note of the dominant chord (scale degrees 5, 7 or 2) is likely to finish with an imperfect cadence. It is the only possible cadence if the last note is 7 or 2, but an ending on the dominant note could be supported by a perfect cadence instead, as shown by cadence (iv) above.

An imperfect cadence always ends on chord V, and in a minor key this requires a raised leading note to ensure that the chord has a major 3rd. However, you have some choice over the first chord of the cadence, as we saw on page 39.

Where the melody ends with scale degrees 1–2, 3–2 or 8–7 the chords are usually I–V or Ib–V. The progression VI–V is another possibility (although it won't work for 3–2 because it results in consecutive 5ths between the outer parts). Other alternatives for 8–7 include IVb–V (called a **phrygian cadence** if in a minor key), IV–V and VI–V. Chords to use when an imperfect cadence ends on a weak beat are discussed on the next page.

Ex. 7.3.4

F major: I   V | G major: Ib   V | A minor: i   V | C major: vi   V

(phrygian cadence)

F major: I   V | D major: IV   V | D minor: ivb   V | A major: vi   V

An imperfect cadence that ends on a weak beat is often harmonised with Ic–V, a progression that will fit melodies ending 3-2, 5-5 or 8-7. The cadential $\frac{6}{4}$ (chord Ic) in this progression is essentially a decoration of chord V rather than a completely independent chord – the 6th and 4th above the bass sound rather like accented non-chord notes and resolve respectively to the 5th and 3rd of chord V. Here are some examples of imperfect cadences using a cadential $\frac{6}{4}$:

Ex. 7.3.5

For more on the cadential $\frac{6}{4}$ see **sections 3.7** and **3.9**.

Finally, here are some common progressions to use for an imperfect cadence when the last note of a phrase is the dominant:

Ex. 7.3.6

Plagal cadences

Plagal cadences are far less common than perfect and imperfect cadences, but can be used for the melodic patterns 4-3, 6-5 and 8-8. Notice that the last cadence in the example below includes a tierce de Picardie on the final chord. As explained in **Section 3.19**, using the major version of the tonic triad is an option for the last chord in a perfect or plagal cadence at the end of a passage in a minor key.

Ex. 7.3.7

Once you have chosen your cadences, sketch in their bass notes and label them with their key(s) and chords. If there is similar motion between melody and bass, watch out for consecutive 5ths or octaves, as defined in **Section 4.3**. These are particularly likely to occur between root-position chords that are a step apart, such as in the vi–V progression shown right.

If consecutives do arise, try inverting one of the chords or changing it to a different chord that still produces the type of cadence you want – you can see

Ex. 7.3.8

from the many examples in this section that there is often plenty of choice. In the second example 7.3.8 on the previous page, the first chord has been changed from vi to I, avoiding consecutive 5ths and producing strong contrary motion with the melody. Remember to alter the chord labelling if you make any changes.

Activity 7.3

a Choose suitable chords for each of the following cadences, which are all in the key of A major. Add the scale degree numbers above the melody notes, label the chords you have chosen and write in the bass notes. Notes in brackets should be regarded as passing notes.

b Choose suitable chords for each of the following cadences, which are all in the key of E minor. Add the scale degree numbers above the melody notes, label the chords you have chosen and write in the bass notes. The note in brackets should be regarded as a passing note.

7.4 Harmonising the approach to a cadence

Perfect cadences

In **Section 3.6** we learned that a perfect cadence is commonly approached from a chord in the subdominant group (IV or ii). It can also be approached from chord I, Ib or Ic – the choice obviously depends on what will fit the given melody.

Cadences (i) – (iii) below show how chord ii can be used as an approach chord:

Ex. 7.4.1

These patterns will also work, with some rearrangement of inner parts, for melodies that end 2-2-3, or they can be used for interrupted cadences by replacing the final tonic chord with chord vi (but remember that interrupted cadences are not common).

The first chord of example (iii) includes a dissonant 7th (the alto G marked with an arrow). Similarly, the first chord of example (iv) includes a dissonant 4th above the bass (again, the alto G). In traditional styles of harmony, these dissonances should be prepared in the chord before. The dissonance should also resolve by falling by step (as it does in both of these examples above).

The following music example shows four choices of approach chord for melodies that end with the common melodic pattern 8–7–8:

Ex. 7.4.2

It is usually best to avoid using chord I *in root position* as an approach chord to a perfect cadence because this can weaken its subsequent impact as the final chord of the phrase. However, chord Ib can provide a good approach to a perfect cadence: see Example 7.4.2 (i) above.

Chord Ic is a valid choice, providing that it falls on a stronger beat than V, as shown in cadence (ii) above. This is because chord Ic shares the same bass note as chord V and 'leans' onto that chord, strengthening its dominant effect. Ic is not a truly independent chord, as we learned in **Section 3.7**, so the approach to a cadential $^6_4$ is really the chord before Ic. Usually, any chord that sounds good before chord V will also be effective before Ic, so possible progressions include IVb–Ic–V–I and iib–Ic–V–I.

There are, of course, many other melodic patterns that form a perfect cadence, but at least one of the approach chords outlined in Examples 7.4.1 and 7.4.2 is likely to work well before most perfect cadences. Note that the final chord I of perfect cadences such as those in Examples 7.4.1 and 7.4.2 (i)–(iii) is capable of being replaced with chord vi, to make an interrupted cadence. (Example 7.4.2 (iv) is an exception, because vi-V-vi would be a poor progression.) However, don't forget that interrupted cadences are not common. You can sometimes use V[7] instead of V in perfect cadences. The 7th is best prepared in the previous chord or approached by step from above, and then must be resolved downwards by step.

Imperfect cadences

Whereas the first chord of a perfect cadence is always V[(7)], the first chord of an imperfect cadence can be I or Ib, ii or iib, IV or IVb, or vi. It is therefore not easy to generalise about suitable approach chords, but here are some examples:

Ex. 7.4.3

Notice again that if you include a cadential $^6_4$, it should be on a stronger beat than chord V, as shown in cadence (viii) of Example 7.4.3.

If the penultimate melody note of a phrase is the same as the one before it, as in cadences (iii) and (v) of Example 7.4.3 and the cadences in Example 7.4.1, it is usually best to harmonise them with two different chords. However, the same chord can be used twice in succession if there is some additional interest, such as the 4–3 suspension on chord V in the last cadence of Example 7.4.1. Sometimes, two different positions of the same chord work well together, such as I–Ib–V to form an imperfect cadence.

This section has so far concentrated on cadential approaches in *major* keys. Minor keys involve a few issues which will come up in **Activity 7.4** (especially in the last part of (a)).

■ Note 7 of a minor key almost always needs to be raised by a semitone in chord V (e.g. V in G minor is D–F♯–A rather than D–F♮–A)

■ The chord on the supertonic is most commonly diminished (*ii*), rather than minor (ii) as in the major key. For example, *ii* in G minor is frequently A–C–E♭ rather than A–C–E. Diminished chords are not often used in root-position, so that Example 7.4.1 (i) is an unlikely pattern in a minor key (whereas *ii*b and *ii⁷*b do both commonly precede V)

■ If you use *ii*b before V, avoid the interval of the augmented 2nd (for example, E♭–F♯ in G minor). In Example 7.4.1 (ii) this interval will occur if you replace the E♮ in the alto with E♭, and then move to the inevitable F♯. Note 6 of the minor scale is sometimes raised, and in this example a minor ii with E♮ will work.

Activity 7.4

a Play or rewrite some of the cadences in Examples 7.4.1 to 7.4.3 in other major keys, such as a tone lower in F major or a tone higher in A major. You could, if you wish, concentrate on just the outer parts, missing out the alto and tenor lines. Then play or rewrite some of the cadences in G *minor* and in other minor keys. Be careful with Example 7.4.1 (i) and (ii): avoid diminished chords in root position, and/or augmented 2nds in the alto. Example 7.4.3 (iii) works well if you make the ii in G major a *ii⁷* (with alto G) in G minor. Use of a minor ii with E♮ would not work here.

b Harmonise each of the following as cadences with approach chords in the named keys. Write the scale degree numbers of the melodies above the upper staves before adding Roman numerals and a bass part on the lower staves. Avoid using Ic in this exercise as we shall be focusing on that chord in the next question.

B♭ major:

E minor:

c Name the key of each of the following passages and then write in a bass part and chord labels to complete each progression, ending with either a perfect or an imperfect cadence. Each one must include Ic at the place indicated. The first cadence (and possibly the second) could be harmonised in either a major key or a minor key - try both if you feel confident.

(i)

(ii)

(iii)

Ic   Ic   Ic

7.5 Harmonising an entire phrase

Having worked out the chords for the cadence and its approach, we can turn our attention to the rest of the phrase. Although it may seem strange to have tackled the end of the phrase first, it makes sense if you remember that in tonal music, a cadence is a 'goal' to which a phrase proceeds.

The order in which you plan the chords for the rest of the phrase is up to you. Some people prefer to continue to work backwards from the cadence approach chord; others prefer to work forwards from the start, taking care that the new chords lead musically into the cadence that has already been planned. Often, a combination of the two methods works well.

The actual choice of chords will depend on what fits with the melody, but you should always aim for a strong harmonic progression, using the principles outlined in **Sections 3.12–3.14** of this book.

In some exercises the opening few notes of the melody may be fully harmonised, to get you started and to provide a model for you to follow. If you have to harmonise the opening for yourself, aim to establish the key as soon as possible, by using a tonic chord in root position on a strong beat. If the melody starts with an anacrusis, see if the progression V–I (or Vb–I) will fit under the opening notes, as this is always an effective way to establish a key.

Here's a method for harmonising a short but complete phrase. The first three chords are given, so there are only four chords to add:

Freylinghausen's *Gesangbuch* (1704) (adapted)

Ex. 7.5.1

Step 1: Identify the key

The key is D major. The key signature points to D major or B minor. The first chord is D major, the last note is D and the note A is always A♮, not A♯ – all features that point to D major, not B minor.

Step 2: Write out a chord diagram and label any given chords

Ex. 7.5.2

Incidentally, you can now use only upper-case Roman numerals if you no longer need to be reminded which triads are major, minor and diminished. However, some people prefer to continue to use lower-case for minor chords and italic lower-case for diminished – it is entirely a matter of choice.

Step 3: Choose suitable chords for the cadence

Here, the given cadence notes are scale degrees 2–1 (E–D in the melody). These will support a perfect cadence in D major. Sketch in the necessary bass notes and label the chords, as shown below:

Ex. 7.5.3

Notice that we have used a low A for chord V, so that the bass can rise in contrary motion to the tune. But all notes should be regarded as provisional until the exercise nears completion, since some may need to be changed once other chords are added.

Step 4: Add a cadence approach chord

The melody note before the cadence is another E, so it could also be harmonised by chord V. However, in **Section 7.4** we learned that it is a good idea to introduce some variety if you use the same chord twice in succession. Here, you could use chord V with a 4–3 suspension, as shown in Example 7.5.4 (a) below.

However, chord ii would also fit the soprano E and, since it works well as a cadence approach chord, that is what we have chosen here. In fact, the chord we have used in Example 7.5.4 (b) is actually ii⁷b, which always forms a musically interesting approach to a perfect cadence. As with a V⁴⁻³ suspension, the dissonant note (D) will need to be prepared on the previous beat and resolved by falling a step to the next beat, and our preliminary draft shows that this is possible:

Ex. 7.5.4 (a)

Ex. 7.5.4 (b)

Step 5: Choose chords for the remaining unharmonised notes

There is now only one more chord to choose, but it needs to follow on well from the last given chord as well as leading musically to the chord that comes next. The obvious choice for bar 1^4 is chord I, because the preceding chord (Vb) generally moves to I. Chord I will fit the given F♯ in the melody and allow the bass to rise from leading note to tonic (C♯–D). Write in the bass note and label the chord, as shown below:

Ex. 7.5.5

D major: I   IVb   Vb   I   ii⁷b   V   I

In most exercises you will have more than one chord to add at this stage. **Sections 3.12–3.14** indicate some harmonic progressions that are likely to work well.

The melody and bass parts should form a strong harmonic outline. Check that there are no consecutive 5ths or octaves – these are less likely to occur if the bass line is in contrary or oblique motion with the soprano part as frequently as possible. If you do find consecutives, try changing one of the chords from a root position to a first inversion (or vice versa) – or try a different chord.

The final steps involve adding inner parts for alto and tenor. When you first start harmonising melodies, you may prefer to omit this stage until you feel confident in choosing chords and writing a bass part.

Step 6: Add alto and tenor parts and check everything carefully

Using your chord labels as a guide, add alto and tenor parts. Make sure that the first added chord follows on properly from the last given chord. Revise the procedures for spacing and doubling in earlier chapters, especially **Sections 2.15**, **2.16** and **4.2–4.3**.

It is good for inner parts to have a sense of line, although in the short example we have been working on, there is no need to be too ambitious. Good, steady inner parts are best, with few large leaps. You can always add interest with one or two well-placed non-chord notes. In the completed working below there is a passing note in the tenor, and the 7th in chord ii⁷b that we planned earlier is correctly prepared and resolved.

Ex. 7.5.6

D major: I   IVb   Vb   I   ii⁷b   V   I

As you can see, the middle parts mainly stay on the same note or move by step. At the end the alto falls a 3rd, which means that the leading note (C♯) doesn't rise to the tonic – this is perfectly acceptable if you want the full effect of all three notes of the tonic triad in a perfect cadence.

Check all six pairs of parts for consecutives (SA, ST, SB, AT, AB and TB), paying particular attention to the 'join' from the last given chord to your first added chord.

When harmonising a melody there is not a single ideal 'answer' – different workings are almost always possible and it is worth trying out alternative chords to find the ones that will sound best in the context.

7.6 Harmonising an entire phrase in a minor key

We'll go through the method again, this time with a minor-key example:

J Chetham: *Psalms*, 1718 (adapted)

Ex. 7.6.1

Step 1

The key signature suggests either B♭ major or G minor – the presence of F♯, the leading note of G minor, from the outset indicates G minor. The phrase can be harmonised perfectly well in that key throughout. It wouldn't be wrong to move into B♭ major for the last two bars, but modulations rarely happen so close to the start, and in a short exercise like this, a change of key is not necessary.

Step 2

Label the given chords, as shown in Example 7.6.2 below. In the bass of bar 1, E♭ is an upper auxiliary and, more importantly, C is likely to be a passing note – which means that the first bass note of bar 2 will need to be B♭.

Step 3

Turning to the cadence, we see that the soprano ends on the dominant, strongly suggesting an imperfect cadence. The melody notes 4–5 in G minor would support the progression ivb–V (a phrygian imperfect cadence). Can you spot why beginning with iv in root position, rather than ivb, would cause a problem?

Step 4

The approach to a phrygian cadence is often from chord i. This will work well, given the soprano B♭ at the start of bar 3.

Step 5

We now just have to decide on the chords for bar 2. We have already concluded that the bass note on the first beat is B♭. When added to the G in the given soprano part, the only possible chord at the start of bar 2 is ib.

The soprano A at the end of bar 2 could carry chord *viib* – a chord often used between the root position and first inversion of the tonic chord. This normally means that as the soprano rises (G–A–B♭) the bass could fall (B♭–A–G), creating some highly desirable contrary motion between the outer parts. But as you can see from our outline working below, the bass actually has an awkward upward leap of a 7th to the first note of bar 3:

Ex. 7.6.2

G minor: i   V _____   ib   *viib*   i   ivb   V

One possible way round this problem is to let the bass descend to a low G and then rise an octave to the upper G, which becomes an additional harmony note, as shown in Example 7.6.3 (a) below.

Another solution is to change chord *viib* to chord V, which will lead just as well into chord i at the start of bar 3. This allows the bass to rise to G through two smaller intervals, as in Example 7.6.3 (b). We have included a passing note in bar 3 which, since the bass is descending, uses F♮ from the descending melodic minor scale:

Ex. 7.6.3 (a)

Ex. 7.6.3 (b)

| ib | viib | i | ivb | V |
| ib | V | i | ivb | V |

Step 6

We'll finish by completing the alto and tenor parts, although you could come back to this step later if you wish. The following shows one way in which this could be done (another can be found in *Hymns Ancient and Modern Revised*, No. 117):

Ex. 7.6.4

G minor: i   V _____   ib   V   i   ivb   V

For clarity, all of the notes we have added are shown in small print above. Notice how just a little melodic decoration (passing notes in the alto at bar 2^2 and bass at bar 3^2) keeps the music moving at points where the other parts have minims.

This example also reminds us of several important points about minor keys:

- In a minor key the *raised* form of the leading note needs to be used:
  - If a part is ascending to the tonic (alto, bars 2^3–3^1)
  - In chord V, when it is followed by chord i (bars 1^3 and 2^3) or when it is the last chord of an imperfect cadence (bar 4).

  Forgetting to raise the leading note in a minor key is a common mistake in exams, so check your own minor-key exercises very carefully.

- Be prepared to raise note 6 of a minor scale when it is followed by the raised version of note 7 – the alto in bar 2^2 needs to be E♮, since E♭ would have resulted in a very awkward augmented 2nd between E♭ and the following F♯

- Be prepared to use the lowered versions of notes 7 and 6 when a part is descending stepwise, as in the bass of bar 3.

In fact, we have both forms of the melodic minor scale in this example. The alto rises through the *ascending melodic minor scale* in bars 2–3: D–E♮–F♯–G. This is nicely balanced in bar 3 by the bass falling through the *descending melodic minor* scale: G–F♮–E♭–D. Revise **Section 1.6** if you feel unsure about melodic minor scales.

Remember that the final stage is to check everything, especially for consecutives: all is well here. Only chords i, V and iv are used, but the two first-inversion chords and the passing notes are very positive features. Short exercises can be successful with a simple chord scheme, provided that inversions are used, part-writing is correct and there are one or two non-chord notes.

A note on adding inner parts

Activity 7.6 includes a number of practice exercises for you to complete. In the early stages you may wish to add just a bass part and chord labels, but make sure that you also complete the full SATB texture as soon as you feel ready.

When adding inner parts in traditional four-part harmony, remember that you will need to:

- Double (or sometimes omit) appropriate chord notes (see **Sections 2.15–2.16**)
- Space chords so that there is no more than an octave between neighbouring parts (except between tenor and bass, where a tenor part high above the bass is fine)
- Write alto and tenor parts that move mainly by step (or repeat the previous note), with occasional *small* leaps for variety
- Add occasional melodic decoration, such as passing notes, especially where the melody lacks rhythmic interest, although *not* after the last chord of a cadence
- Check that you have avoided the parallel intervals described in **Section 4.3**.

Activity 7.6

Complete the harmonisation of each of the following passages and label all of the chords in each one.

a   The minim A *could* be accompanied by minims in the other parts, but some rhythmic variety is better, either by using a suspension, or by writing two different chords under the minim A. Try both solutions.

Melody by Martin Luther

b

W Horsley: *Horsley* (hymn tune)

c   Think carefully about the key of this extract, noticing that there is neither C♯ nor C♮ in the given music.

Melody from *Nürnbergisches Gesangbuch*, 1676

d When the time signature indicates that the beat is a minim, melodic decoration will usually be written in crotchets. This melody includes several non-chord notes around which you will need to plan your harmonies.

Handel: *Cannons* (adapted)

New Universal Psalmodist, 1770 (adapted)

e

G J Elvey: Psalm chant

f

Melody from James Green's *Book of Psalmody* (1724)

g

H Benham

h

H Benham

i

8 Harmonising a melody – longer examples

8.1 A reminder: melody and bass

Remember, as you start this new chapter, that the most important ingredients of tonal harmony are still melody and bass.. Between them, they define the key and the chords. A good bass part tends to be more angular than the other parts because the need to outline strong harmony often results in leaps of a 4th or 5th between root-position chords. Nevertheless, when writing a bass part we must still think about the horizontal aspect of the music and build a firm but strong line to underpin purposeful chord progressions.

8.2 Harmonising longer melodies

The method is broadly the same as that outlined in **Section 7.5**, but there may be more than one key to identify in a longer passage of music, and there will certainly be more than one cadence to deal with. In longer exercises, identification of keys in Step 1 must go hand-in-hand with identifying where the cadences come, which in turn will depend on the phrase structure.

Example 8.2.1 below is a hymn tune composed by S S Wesley, a leading composer from the early Victorian era. The given notes suggest that the bass will move chiefly in crotchets, but we can add a little quaver movement where appropriate. In a bass part this is usually achieved by adding passing notes. The commas indicate phrase endings – where the cadences will come (as explained in Step 1 below).

Ex. 8.2.1   S S Wesley: *Wigan*

Step 1

The key signature suggests B♭ major or G minor. The presence of F♯ in the first phrase and the ending on G confirms that the overall key is G minor.

D minor (the dominant of G minor) is indicated by the E♮–D in bars 7-8. C minor (the subdominant) is indicated by the C–B♮–C in bar 10. Somewhat unusually, everything appears to be minor, without the almost expected modulation to the relative major, B♭.

Step 2

Unless you are already confident at working out chords in different keys, make yourself chord diagrams for all three keys required: G minor, D minor and C minor. We also need to label the given chords, as shown in Example 8.2.2 *opposite*. Notice that the implied chord at bar 1³ is V⁷c – chord *ii* might have seemed more obvious, but it would not sound good after Vb on the previous beat.

Step 3

Now we need to work out chords for the five cadences. Four of them are perfect, which should not be surprising, because perfect cadences are very common in traditional harmony.

The exception is in bar 12, where an imperfect cadence will fit the semitone descent from
B♭ to A (scale degrees 3–2 in G minor). There are other possibilities, such as an imperfect
cadence in B♭ major or a plagal cadence in F major, although Wesley himself used minor keys
throughout, probably because the words of verse 1 of the hymn are all dark and serious.

Two important tips to note:

- The fall of a semitone at the end of a phrase usually signifies an *imperfect* cadence.

- Forgetting the key signature may cause you to miscalculate important intervals. At bars
  12[2-3], we hear a semitone, not a tone, because the melody falls from B♭ to A, not from B to A.
  The latter would imply a perfect cadence in A minor, which would be unlikely in a piece that
  is about to end in G minor.

Step 4

Having decided on the cadences, we can choose cadence approach chords, and label all of
the harmonies we have added so far:

Ex. 8.2.2

Step 5

Perhaps surprisingly – certainly pleasingly – almost half of the chords have now been planned.

There are several points to bear in mind when filling the gaps:

- Where possible, a modulation should be preceded by a **pivot chord** (see page 46) to
  smooth the transition from one key to the next

- It is fine to begin a new phrase by repeating the chord heard at the end of the previous
  phrase, but the harmonisation will be more interesting if the chord changes from a root
  position to a first inversion or vice versa, or if the bass leaps an octave, as in bars 4[4] and 10[4]
  of Example 8.2.3 on the next page

- Aim for a good mix of root-position and first-inversion chords: progressions such as i–Vb,
  Vb–i, ib–V and V–ib can provide welcome variety in the earlier part of phrases when entirely
  root-position versions of tonic and dominant chords have been used at cadence points.

There are often lots of possible chords to choose from, so no two people are likely to finish
Step 5 with exactly the same bass part and implied chords. Our own suggestion follows on
the next page, but Wesley himself included two diminished 7th chords (in bars 11[2] and 12[2]),
perhaps to provide tension in this climactic phrase, whereas our harmony is less ambitious.

Wesley's original setting is in *Hymns Ancient and Modern Revised*, No. 212.

Notice that we have made a few refinements to the chords originally planned on the previous page. Chord iv on the first beat of bar 10 would have been fine, but there is a splendid opportunity to use *ii⁷b* here, because the 7th (C) is already prepared in the given melody on the last beat of bar 9 and resolves by falling by step to B♮ on the second beat of bar 10.

We have also included some passing notes and, since the one added in bar 12 (F♯) would have resulted in an augmented 2nd (E♭–F♯) in the bass line, the sixth degree of the scale has been raised from E♭ to E♮, resulting in the major version of chord IV at the start of bar 12. Also, 4-♯3 suspensions have been suggested to provide movement beneath the soprano minims in bars 7³⁻⁴ and 13³⁻⁴.

Ex. 8.2.3

Step 6

The last stage is to add inner parts. If you feel ready, try this using the chords we have planned and the following opening:

Ex. 8.2.4

Vb i V____ ib_____ i   v⁷d ib V i ivb
        D minor: iv   ic   V⁴⁻³ i   C minor: ib

G minor: iv V IVb i V ib iv i V⁴⁻³ i
ii⁷b V i_____   VI V i

Notice that the bass part frequently moves in contrary motion to the melody and that pivot chords are labelled in terms of both the previous key and the new key.

Finally, check all six pairs of parts for consecutives and make sure that you have used the correct accidentals for scale degrees 6 (E♭ or E♮) and 7 (F or F♯) throughout.

8.3 Checking your work

Most of the information you need on such matters as doubling and omitting notes, spacing chords and avoiding consecutives, is available in **Sections 2.15, 2.16, 4.2** and **4.3**. The following music example (a deliberately faulty completion of Example 8.2.4) has been devised to allow you to spot various kinds of things that are likely to occur in longer passages of four-part harmony. Not every mistake is mentioned in the commentary that follows – we have left some for you to find in **Activity 8.3**.

Ex. 8.3

a Consecutive octaves between alto and bass, and a doubled leading note (F♯) in the second chord. Giving the alto A rather than F♯ would correct this.

b Consecutive octaves between soprano and tenor, and consecutive perfect 5ths between soprano and alto. Both problems can be solved by sharpening the F in the alto part (a perfect 5th followed by a diminished 5th is fine in upper parts) and by giving the tenor D in the second chord.

c The start of an extremely monotonous alto part – more variety in pitch is needed.

d Judging from the melody, two syllables are to be sung in this bar. The bass can share its four notes between two syllables easily enough, but what are the alto and tenor supposed to do?

e The gap between alto and tenor is too wide and contributes to the awkwardly angular tenor part in bar 10. There is also an **overlap** on beat 2, caused by the bass being higher than the tenor on the previous beat. Chord spacing and/or note doubling needs replanning in this bar. Note that there is no problem with the overlap on beat 4 of bar 10 because this is the start of a new phrase.

There is more about overlapping in the *A Level Music Harmony Workbook 2*.

f The third (E♮) is not the best note to double in a major chord – doubling the 5th would be a better choice here, thus giving G to the alto. Notice that between beats 2 and 3 of this bar, an opportunity has been missed for the alto to sing passing notes in parallel 3rds with the tenor. A quaver E♮ between the alto's D and F♯ would sound very effective.

g The suspension in the alto has not been prepared. Either it should have been given to the tenor (whose G at bar 13² could prepare it), or there should be correct preparation in the alto.

h F♯ to E♭ is an augmented 2nd. Augmented intervals are awkward to sing and are best avoided in four-part vocal harmony. It is also not common practice to put a passing note between the leading note and dominant in a perfect cadence, even when it doesn't involve an augmented 2nd.

i It is usually preferable not to decorate the final chord of a perfect cadence and here the tenor's suspension is not well handled. The quaver C at bar 13⁴ which prepares the suspension is only a passing note. In a suspension, preparation is usually from a harmony note, and preferably one which is at least as long as the dissonance it precedes.

Activity 8.3

a There are yet more problems in Example 8.3. Describe each of the four errors marked * in the music on page 107.

b Example 8.3 ends with a tierce de Picardie. What does this term mean?

c Name the key of the passage below, complete the bass part and label all of the chords. Add inner parts as soon as you feel confident to do so.

The music, which is a 19th-century hymn tune, has a minim beat, making the music look slower and more solemn than it need be in modern performance. The first five phrases are eight minims in length; the final phrase is 12 minims long. All phrases begin with a minim anacrusis. The modulation in the second phrase is very clear, but there's at least one implied modulation later. Notice how the 7th (F in the alto part) at the start of bar 2 is prepared on the previous beat and resolves by falling to E on the second beat of bar 2. Above this, the crotchet A in the soprano part is an échappée.

d Add a vocal bass part and chord symbols to the following melody. Also complete the inner parts as soon as you feel confident to do so.

The four-bar phrasing of this melody should be clear from the presence of the dotted minims in the melody, which mark the ends of each of the four phrases. What may not be quite so obvious is the implied modulation in the second phrase: F♯ in bar 7 is no longer the leading note, because it does not rise to the tonic.

H S Oakfield: *Abends*

Plenty of additional practice material for four-part harmonisation can be found in any traditional hymn book. Work from a melody-only edition if possible so that you are not influenced by the original harmonies, and later compare your own working with the harmonisation given in a full-music edition of the same hymn book.

9 Some other textures

This chapter introduces you to some types of texture other than the 'hymn tune' style that we have been working with until this point. We shall learn a little about writing for single voice with accompaniment, for keyboard, and for three or four instruments.

Important differences from the 'hymn tune' style include the following:

- A much greater pitch range is available when writing for instruments
- The harmonic pace will generally be slower, often with only one chord per bar, or even the same chord lasting for several bars, rather than one chord per beat
- When completing the texture, the layout will need to suit the characteristics of the instrument(s) concerned, perhaps by splitting harmony notes into broken chords or by repeating notes in patterns (called **figuration**)
- Bass parts may be doubled in octaves. Non-chord notes may be treated freely (so that, for example, a dissonance might resolve in a different octave or perhaps after some intervening pitches).

In this chapter we discuss some of the issues involved in a small selection of the various textures that you could use.

9.1 Songs

We start with a song that remains in the same key throughout and can be harmonised with simple chords:

Stephen Foster: *The Old Folks at Home*

The song ends by repeating the melody of bars 5–8. We'll apply our by now familiar series of steps to create a bass part and chord symbols for this tune.

Step 1

The key is clearly D major throughout.

Step 2

Label the harmonies in the first three bars, having first made a chord diagram for D major if you need one. The chords are I–IVc–I. Note the style of this opening so that you can continue it in your own work. There is only one chord per bar, with the bass note sounded (in octaves) on the first beat and the rest of the chord played three times by the right hand on the remaining three beats.

You should not necessarily expect there to be only one chord in every bar – it is common in many types of music for the rate of harmonic change to increase on the approach to a cadence. However, the given opening certainly suggests that chords do not need to change very frequently in this song.

Step 3

Cadence points are also clear, since there is a rest in the vocal part after each phrase. Chord V is the obvious choice for bar 4, as it will harmonise the E and form an imperfect cadence (I–V) in conjunction with the given chord in the previous bar.

The melody ends on the tonic in bar 8, suggesting a perfect cadence. Chord V will fit under the Es in the second half of bar 7 but it will not support the whole bar, since the melody on the first two beats outlines a tonic triad.

The melody in bar 11 outlines chord IV, and the A in bar 12 could be harmonised by a tonic chord, resulting in a plagal cadence (IV– I). In fact, that is exactly what the composer wrote, perhaps because the gentle sound of a plagal cadence suits the nostalgic mood of the words. However, it is not the only possibility. Because bar 12 leads back to a repeat of the main tune, we have decided to prepare for that return by using an imperfect cadence (ii^7–V) in bars 11^3–12. Chord ii^7 works well here because its 7th (D) can be prepared in the chord before (which has to include the melody note D) and it can resolve in bar 12 by falling to C♯ as part of chord V.

Step 4

We need an approach chord in the first half of bar 7 to lead into the perfect cadence. The melody outlines the notes of chord I, but a root-position tonic chord here would detract from its appearance in bar 8. Ib is possible, but the best choice would be Ic, since this chord has the dominant note in the bass which will strengthen the effect of the perfect cadence that follows.

The approach chord for the first half of bar 11 must support the notes D and B in the melody and lead into the ii^7–V progression we have already decided upon for the actual cadence. Chords IV, IVb and vi would all do: we have chosen IVb.

Step 5

We now need to fill in the remaining chords. Sometimes in a song there is obvious melodic repetition. In our example, bars 5–6 are a repeat of bars 1–2. When dealing with simple melodies a safe option is to reuse the previous chords. But it is often more enterprising to introduce some kind of variation. One possibility would be to use chord IV in root position instead of second inversion in bar 6, leading into it with a passing note in the previous bar. Another would be to use some minor chords – perhaps ii in the second half of bar 5 followed by vi in bar 6.

The melody in bar 9 outlines chord V (with a passing note on D) and this would lead naturally to chord Ib in bar 10, perhaps via another passing note. We have chosen Ib for bar 10 because I in root position has been used enough already in the first eight bars.

At this stage you should play through your working and check carefully that there are no mistakes. Even in an accompanied song, there should not be any consecutive 5ths or octaves between the bass and the vocal melody. This is also the time to see if the working can be improved by, for example, including some simple melodic decoration. In Example 9.1.2 (on the next page) we have added some brief melodic ideas to the bass in bars 4, 8 and 12. These are all places where the singer has a long note and a rest, and are therefore good moments to focus interest on the bass to move the music forwards. Notice that the bass figure in bar 4 is derived from the opening bar of the melody, while the bass in bar 12 hints at the singer's notes heard in bar 9. Here is the outline harmonisation we have decided upon in our five steps:

Ex. 9.1.2

D major: I — IVc — I — V ———

I ——— IVb — IV — Ic — V — I ———

V ——— (7) — Ib — I ——— (♮7) — IVb — ii⁷ — V ———

One further refinement has been suggested above at the end of bar 10. Adding a chromatic passing note on C♮ creates a chord of D⁷ (D–F♯–A–C♮) at this point, which not only leads effectively into the G major first inversion on the next beat, but also adds a touch of chromatic colour to the pause chord.

Activity 9.1.1

Complete the bass and add chord symbols to the following extract from a song. There is a possible modulation to a related key in bars 6–8, but this is not essential.

There is also a two-bar melodic sequence in the song and it will sound very effective if it is supported by a bass and chords that also repeat in sequence. For example, if the progression I–IV is repeated a step higher in sequence, it will become ii–V. For more on harmonic sequences, see page 42.

Air 53 from *The Beggar's Opera* (1728)

One wife — is too much for most hus - bands to hear, but two — at — a —

time there's no mor - tal can bear. This way, and — that way, and which way I ____ will, What would com - fort the ___ one t'oth - er wife would take ill.

Example 9.1.2 above shows just a bass part and chord symbols. We will now develop those into a complete texture, using the opening three bars as a model. (This is, in fact, the final stage of the six-step method begun on pages 110–111). The composer, Stephen Foster, kept to the model of the opening bars throughout his accompaniment, and that is perfectly acceptable if done well. However, the working in Example 9.1.3 goes a little further, while still maintaining the style of the opening.

Notice that:

- The accompaniment supports the voice but doesn't just double the melody
- The harmonic changes we introduced to create variety in the second phrase are supported by dropping the left-hand octaves and by repeating the singer's rising 3rd in bar 6 in order to take the chords into a higher register, above the voice
- The texture is at its most dense at the end of bar 10, where a five-note chord underpins the pause in the vocal line.

Activity 9.1.2

Identify the key(s) of the following passage, add a bass part (labelling all of the chords) and then complete the piano accompaniment.

Allegro con spirito

Melody by John Shield (after Turlough O'Carolan): *The Arethusa*

Come all — ye jol - ly sail - ors — bold, Whose hearts are cast in hon - our's mould, While

Eng - lish glo - ry I un - fold; Hur - rah, — for the A - re - thu - sa!

9.2 Keyboard pieces

The following keyboard piece modulates to the dominant in bars 6–8, returning abruptly to the tonic in bar 9 when E♭ returns in the left hand:

Ex. 9.2.1

Haydn, Minuet, Hob. IX:3/3

B♭ major: I   *viib*   *vii*   I   Vb
                                              F major: Ib

viib   Vb   I   Ic   V   I   B♭ major: V⁷d   Ib

V⁷b   I   IV   Ib   iib   Ic   V   I

The chords are simple, with one harmony per bar except where the harmonic rhythm quickens on the approach to the two main cadences. But the melody demonstrates an important characteristic of late 18th-century writing – a fondness for accented dissonances (marked * in the melody).

When faced with a melody note that doesn't seem to fit with its surroundings, look at the *next* note to see if this could be the resolution of a dissonance, and therefore the actual harmony note that you will use as the basis for choosing a chord. It rarely sounds good to treat non-chord notes as if they were harmony notes.

The dissonant notes on the third beats of bars 4, 8 and 12 deserve special attention – the left hand is silent when these occur, but they still sound dissonant because the previous bass note tends to be retained in the memory. A similar figure occurs in the first two notes of the melody, but (as is common with an anacrusic start) this first upbeat is left unharmonised.

Notice the rhythm of the bass part – even though many *chords* last for three beats, Haydn re-sounds the notes on each crotchet to energise the dance style. Also take note of the texture, since it will be a useful model when you come to complete your own full-textured exercises. There are never more than three notes at a time, sometimes only two, and Haydn is happy to end both main cadences with bare octaves (bars 8 and 16). When there are three notes, he allocates two to the left hand, mainly in parallel 3rds or 6ths.

Activity 9.2

a Name the key, complete the bass part and label the chords in the following piece.
Think carefully about the A♮ in bar 15: is it likely that a modulation would occur so close to the end? If not, the A♮ is likely to be a chromatic appoggiatura.

Beethoven: Ecossaise, WoO. 86

b Here is another exercise, in a minor key. Complete the bass part and label the chords.

Consider using an imperfect (phrygian) cadence in bars 7–8. Bars 13–16 are a sequence of the previous four bars. Would a harmonic sequence work here?

KEYBOARD PIECES

Rameau: Menuet (*Premier livre de pièces de clavecin*, 1706)

In keyboard music, textures are usually freer than those in vocal writing:

- The number of notes sounding together may vary during the course of the piece
- Different parts can have different rhythms – for example, the bass may be fairly static while the right hand is quite busy
- The parts need not keep to the limited ranges of vocal music.

In spite of this, there are important similarities between keyboard textures in tonal music and four-part vocal textures:

- Inner parts still often tend to favour small intervals
- Consecutive 5ths and octaves are normally avoided, although a bass line or melody may be systematically doubled in octaves as a particular effect
- Dissonances are usually prepared (or at least approached by step) and resolved.

Some types of keyboard music, particularly in the 18th century, are written in two parts throughout (one part for the right hand and the other for the left). Others, such as the *Menuet* by Rameau above, are largely in two parts, but also include a little thickening of the texture to fill out the chords at the main cadences. The texture should not be artificially filled out if the given opening suggests that the piece is predominantly in two parts: in this case two parts are sufficient.

The texture in keyboard music – again, principally in the 18th century – is often lightened by writing the harmonies as **broken chords** rather than block chords. In the following example, the bass line (which starts in the treble clef) is incorporated into the broken-chord patterns so that there is only a two-part texture, with very obvious implied harmonies:

Ex. 9.2.2

Andante

Attwood: Sonata No. 3 in F

D minor: i   V⁷b   i   V   i   V⁷b

9.3 Trios and quartets

If you write for a trio or quartet of instruments, the part for each instrument should be written on its own stave. The notes on all three (or four) staves must be correctly aligned above each other.

Any parts for transposing instruments should normally be written in the appropriate key. For example, a part for B♭ clarinet will normally be notated a tone higher than it sounds – in D major if the key of any non-transposing instruments is C major: see the Reference section for more information.

On writing for string quartet, see *A Level Music Harmony Workbook 2*.

When writing for a small ensemble, make good use of the range of each instrument and try to maintain melodic interest in each of the parts.

Music for trio or quartet varies a great deal in texture. Some is mainly note-against-note, like Example 9.3.1 below, in which the two upper parts are often in parallel 3rds above a simpler bass part.

Ex. 9.3.1

Allegro

Mozart: Divertimento No. 2 for Three Basset Horns, K.Anh. 229

Clarinet 1

Clarinet 2

Bassoon

F major: I ____   V⁷ ____   Ib   iib   V   Ib   viib   I   V⁷

Other pieces may be more contrapuntal, like the texture shown in the next example, which includes expressive suspensions in the second violin part and changes of chord on every beat:

Ex. 9.3.2

Andantino

Pergolesi: Trio Sonata No. 3 in G

Violin 1

Violin 2

Cello

E minor: i   viib   ib   iv   ib   ii⁷   ic   V   i   iv   ib   ii⁷   ic   V   i

Activity 9.3

Complete the bass, name the key, and label all the chords in the following passage. Then add a middle part, much of which could well be in crotchets. Dotted minims in bars 8 and 20 will reinforce the cadences at these points.

The lack of an F♯ between bars 5 and 14 is a strong indication that much of this section is in the relative major. There is also a brief modulation to the subdominant in bars 16–17.

Handel: Menuet from *The Water Music*

10 Figured bass

We referred to figured bass briefly in Chapter 8. We now look at it in some detail because

- **you will encounter it when you are studying Baroque music**
- **you may come across it in some types of harmony and counterpoint exercises.**

10.1 Figured bass

A **figured bass** is a bass part (especially in Baroque music) which includes numbers and other symbols (such as sharp and flat signs) below the notes. These numbers and symbols show the types of chords required, enabling a keyboard (or lute) player to improvise an accompaniment for other fully-notated parts – in other words to **realise** a figured bass.

Figured bass works in terms of **intervals above the bass**, using the scale of the current key. So, in Example 10.1 the figures $^6_4$ indicate that a 6th and a 4th above G are required to complete the chord, thus making a $^6_4$ chord of C major. The player has considerable freedom to adapt the realisation to the context, providing that the basic chord is correct. The notes may be put in different octaves, some may be doubled, the chord might be arpeggiated, and passing notes and other types of melodic decoration might be improvised to link a progression of chords.

Ex. 10.1

10.2 Figured bass: using numbers

Baroque composers and players were so familiar with figured bass that abbreviated figuring was employed whenever possible. In particular, the figures 5 and 3 were not used unless needed for clarification. So, where a $^5_3$ (the most common type of chord) was required, no figures at all were shown unless accidentals were involved.

In practice, Baroque composers went further. They tended to rely on a player's ability to recognise what chords were needed *from the bass part alone*, and therefore often used figures only where there might be any uncertainty. However, in harmony exercises, as in some modern editions of Baroque music, basses are normally figured fully enough to show exactly what chords are required.

Widely-used figurings are listed in the following table. The first column shows the abbreviated figuring, which is what you should normally expect to see. The second column shows the full figuring, and the third column gives descriptions and examples (all in close position). You don't need to memorise this table. Provided you know your intervals and keys, and understand how figuring is abbreviated, you can always work out the required notes directly from the figured bass part. Where two or more figures are required the higher/highest number is always written at the top, in descending order.

(nothing)	$^5_3$	triad in root position	
6	$^6_3$	triad in first inversion	
$^6_4$	$^6_4$	triad in second inversion	
7	$^7_5_3$	7th chord in root position	
$^6_5$	$^6_5_3$	7th chord in first inversion	
$^4_3$	$^6_4_3$	7th chord in second inversion	
$^4_2$	$^6_4_2$	7th chord in third inversion	

4 3	5 5 / 4 3	4 - 3 suspension with root-position triad
9 8	9 8 / 5 5 / 3 3	9 - 8 suspension with root position triad
7 6	7 6 / 3 3	7 - 6 suspension with first-inversion triad

6 5	6 5 / 3 3	A $\frac{6}{3}$ followed by a $\frac{5}{3}$ over the same bass note. 6 5 does *not* mean the same as $\frac{6}{5}$.
____		A horizontal extension line means that the previous chord is still in operation, even though the bass note has changed.

Activity 10.2

a Add figuring where needed under each of the following chords.

b Add notes above the following bass part to make the chords indicated by the figuring. The first three chords have been completed for you. Aim to give two notes to the right hand in each of your added chords.

10.3 Figured bass: using accidentals

Figuring works in connection with the key signature. The first example below has no figuring, so it must be a $\frac{5}{3}$ chord on E. Since the key signature contains a G♯, the notes of this $\frac{5}{3}$ are E–G♯–B, a triad of E major. The second example does not have a G♯ in its key signature, so this $\frac{5}{3}$ must be E–G–B, a triad of E minor.

Ex. 10.3.1

A major   =   A minor   =

In order to change any pitches dictated by the key signature, accidentals are needed in the figuring. **An accidental by itself alters the 3rd above the bass.** So, in the next two examples, the first chord is E minor and the second is E major.

Ex. 10.3.2

The most common use of an accidental is to accommodate the raised leading note in a minor key, as in Example 10.3.2 (ii) above, where G♯ is the leading note of A minor. If an interval other than the 3rd above the bass requires a sharp, flat or natural, the accidental should precede the interval number.

For instance, in Example 10.3.3 below:

- ♭5 means that the 5th above the bass must be flattened, and
- ♯6 means that the 6th above the bass must be sharpened.

Ex. 10.3.3

Note that in some printed music the accidental is written *after* the numeral (for instance, 6♭ instead of ♭6), or sharpening can be indicated by a slash through a number – for example, 6̸ means the same as ♯6. Also, you may see ♯3, ♮3, or ♭3, rather than an accidental on its own, to indicate an alteration to the 3rd above the bass note.

Activity 10.3

a Write the correct figuring below the stave for each of the following chords.

b Complete a chord in close position over each of the following bass notes to match the following figurings. The first chord is given.

Reference section

Other major and minor keys

The tables of keys and scales on pages 9 and 13 include key signatures of up to four sharps and four flats – the ones most widely encountered. However, it is good to be able to work in other keys, not least because these may occur when there are modulations from 'simpler' keys.

The table below illustrates major and minor keys that were not covered earlier. The first column shows the scale with accidentals before each note that needs them, the second shows the scale with its key signature, and the third shows you how the key signature is written in the bass clef.

B major

G♯ minor (relative minor of B major)

F♯ major

D♯ minor (relative minor of F♯ major)

D♭ major

B♭ minor (relative minor of D♭ major)

G♭ major

E♭ minor (relative minor of G♭ major)

The symbol **✗** before note 7 in the scales of G♯ minor and D♯ minor indicates a double sharp. F**✗** is *two* semitones above F – in other words, the same pitch as G – while C**✗** is *two* semitones above C – the same pitch as D.

In the case of minor keys, only the harmonic minor scale is included in the table opposite. If you need a melodic minor scale, remember that:

- The ascending melodic minor scale differs from the harmonic minor in having a raised note 6.

- The descending melodic minor differs from the harmonic minor in having a lowered note 7. It needs an accidental only when one is necessary to cancel the effect of a raised 7 earlier in the same bar. For instance, in B♭ minor you would only have to write A♭ for the lowered seventh if A♮ had occurred earlier in the bar.

The scales of F♯ major and G♭ major are **enharmonic equivalents**, which means that they sound the same but are notated differently. The scales of D♯ minor and E♭ minor are also enharmonic equivalents.

Which you choose depends on context. In the key of E major, the dominant is B major, and if you needed to modulate to the dominant key of B major, it would be sensible to choose F♯ major because it merely means adding two sharps to the four already present in E major. But in the key of A♭ major, if you wanted to modulate to the subdominant of the subdominant key, it would make more sense to choose G♭ major rather than F♯ major, again because it would involve far fewer accidentals.

Using score-writing software

Score-writing software does not necessarily produce clear and correct notation automatically. You have to be prepared to intervene, and this is not always easy. Take advice from someone who has plenty of experience with the program in question.

In particular avoid:

- Incorrect beaming of short notes and faulty grouping of rests
- Unnecessarily repeated accidentals
- Wrong bar numbering where the music begins with an upbeat (the first *complete* bar should be bar 1)
- Labelling parts wrongly (for example, four-part vocal music is not for piano)
- Cramped or over-generous spacing between staves or within individual bars

However expert you become in using score-writing software, it is still good to learn how to write music by hand accurately, neatly and quickly!

Ranges of voices

It is generally best to keep to the ranges shown below in most types of writing for four-part voices.

Soprano   Alto   Tenor   Bass

Remember that you can often achieve good spacing by keeping the tenor part high (around middle C and above) for much of the time.

Ranges of instruments

Sensible working ranges for some of the more commonly used instruments are listed below. Good players can manage higher notes than those shown here, but you should be cautious about going beyond the ranges indicated by notes in black type.

Parts for transposing instruments such as the clarinet in B♭ are normally written at a different pitch from sounding (or 'concert') pitch. Where two ranges for an instrument are shown, the first shows written pitch, the second shows concert pitch.

Recorder

Notice that the treble recorder cannot play lower than F above middle C. The descant recorder sounds an octave higher than written.

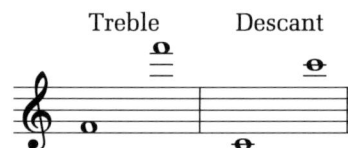

Flute

Be careful not to overuse the lower notes, which tend to be rather quiet. The flute's brightest range extends upwards from D, a 9th above middle C.

Oboe

Avoid rapid passages in the lower part of the register and remember that it is difficult to play quietly on the very lowest notes.

Clarinet in B♭

The clarinet in B♭ is written a tone higher than concert pitch (so that written D sounds as C). There will be an appropriate change of key signature: for example, in a G major piece, a clarinet in B flat will have a key signature of three sharps (for A major) not one sharp (for G major).

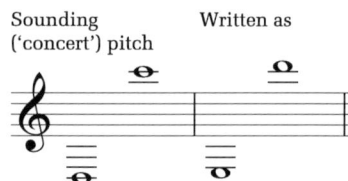

Alto saxophone

The alto saxophone (in E♭) is written a major 6th higher than it sounds.

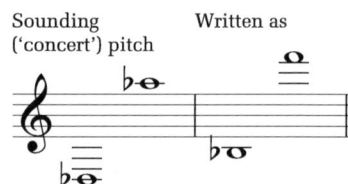

Bassoon

As with the oboe, the lowest notes of the bassoon's range should be used sparingly. The tenor clef (𝄡), which indicates the position of middle C on the fourth line of the stave, is sometimes used for high passages.

Trumpet in B♭

The trumpet in B♭ is written a tone higher than concert pitch (so that written D sounds as C). There will be an appropriate change of key signature: for example, in an F major piece, a trumpet in B♭ will have a key signature of one sharp (for G major) not one flat (for F major). Use the lowest notes sparingly.

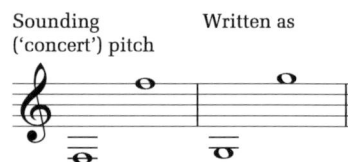

Violin

In trios and quartets (see **Section 9.3**), it is generally best to avoid taking violin parts too low as they may sound dull and may bring the melody uncomfortably close to the bass.

Cello

As with the bassoon, the tenor clef (𝄡), which indicates the position of middle C, is sometimes used for parts that make extensive use of the higher register.

Index

Music credits